THE HOUSE
AT ROYAL OAK

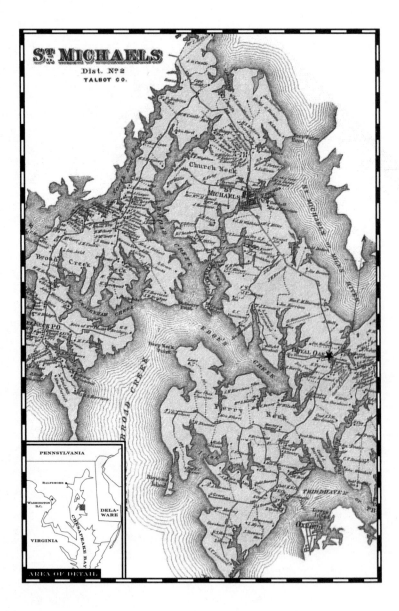

THE HOUSE
AT ROYAL OAK

Starting Over

& Rebuilding a Life

One Room at a Time

CAROL ERON RIZZOLI

BLACK DOG
& LEVENTHAL
PUBLISHERS
NEW YORK

Published by
Black Dog & Leventhal Publishers, Inc.
151 West 19th Street
New York, NY 10011

Distributed by
Workman Publishing Company
225 Varick Street
New York, NY 10014

Manufactured in the United States of America
Interior design by Elizabeth Driesbach
Cover design by Andy Carpenter
Frontispiece map from "The 1877 Atlas of Talbot County,"
Historical Society of Talbot County

ISBN-13: 978-1-57912-840-1

h g f e d c b a

Excerpt from "Eden is that old-fashioned House," by Emily Dickinson, first
published posthumously, in 1914, in *The Single Hound*, compiled by the poet's niece.
Reprinted by permission of the publishers and the Trustees of Amherst College from
The Poems of Emily Dickinson, Thomas H. Johnson, ed., Cambridge, Mass.:
The Belknap Press of Harvard University Press, Copyright © 1951, 1955, 1979,
1983 by the President and Fellows of Harvard College.

Excerpt from "The Floating Aria," by John Barth, copyright © 1994
by John Barth, reprinted by permission of the author.

"The Bookstall," by Linda Pastan, reprinted by permission of the author.

Library of Congress Cataloging-in-Publication
Data available upon request.

THIS BOOK IS DEDICATED
TO FELLOW TRAVELERS, BOOK LOVERS,
AND THE SWEET, SIMPLE FRUITS
OF THE EARTH.

Eden is that old-fashioned House
We dwell in every day
Without suspecting our abode
Until we drive away.

—EMILY DICKINSON

Contents

Prologue

IT BEGINS WITH OPENING THE DOOR TO OTHER PEOPLE, other lives. At times it's like being a flight attendant on a plane that never lands. At other times it's a slow-motion juggling act with the roles of chef, gardener, handyperson, psychologist, marketing specialist, bookkeeper, plumber, and at-ease host all vying for attention, along with unpredictable guests and harrowing encounters—if you settle in the country, as we did—with wildlife and gunfire. It's always . . . interesting, this new life, always a challenge to how you go about things, to how you think, to who you are, and what you may become.

"Our lives are messages, brethren," John Barth writes, "by our bodies embottled, afloat in the great sea of the world. We wash up on other folks' shorelines, they on ours." Professional firefighters, a ballroom dance teacher, a television producer, a police chief, a film critic, an architect, and an art therapist come to this new home of ours—and theirs—along with a feng shui expert, an artist of the surreal, a contractor offering a boxful of antique glass doorknobs from the house he is renovating. A chef arrives with his own crab cakes, salad, bread, and wine to share, and a surgeon who observes, "I would guess that being responsible for the well-being of others weighs on you." Journalists and poets come to stay and a therapist specializing in travel anxiety. On arriving, a decoy dealer spots my yard-sale duck. "I can tell you who carved it, and when," he says. "By the way, you might want to bring it in from the porch."

Of almost a thousand visitors who have come and stayed so far, the one I see as emblematic—the quintessential visitor with a message—is the guest horticulturist. Opening the doors to the dining room one early Sunday morning, I was surprised to see her already there, kneeling on a folded rectangle of newspaper. My first thought was that she was praying.

Next to her I noticed my bottle of dish detergent and paper towels. Pin neat in a pleated plaid skirt and white blouse, her white hair clipped short, she, through absolutely no fault of her own, made me feel remiss. Engrossed in cleaning something, she didn't hear me come in. I set down the coffee tray and said good morning.

"Handsome Areca palm," she said without looking up. "But you've got quite a nasty case of scale here." I'd noticed something, I said lamely, but didn't want to spray it with chemicals.

"Of course not. But scale will kill your plant and it will spread to your other plants. I can tell you how to get completely rid of it, however. Wipe dish soap on the leaves and stems and pour soapy water into the soil." She looked up. "Be sure to do it every week for a month."

I thanked her, once again having learned something from a guest. She wasn't finished either. Palms, she said, are so-named because of their lovely resemblance to the human hand.

Guests come to this home away from home, a bed-and-breakfast, to celebrate an anniversary, a wedding, a birthday, a family reunion. They come for business, for trysts, to consider life transitions, and to recover from them. They come to house hunt, to goose hunt, to escape from houseguests, to get engaged, to honeymoon, to start a family, to get away for a romantic weekend without the kids. Others come to shop, bicycle, sail, kayak, go fishing, take in the sights, sketch, visit art galleries, eat crabs, read. Some just want to practice the fine art of doing nothing, as they say in Italian, *il dolce far niente*. The loose local translation might be "Come sit on the porch."

They come curious, bored, adventurous, tired, delighted to escape "real" life for a day or two. A few are suspicious, wary of the experience at hand. A few are superstitious. On September 11 every year someone from New York or Washington always books a room just to get out of the city.

Long after you're certain you've seen it all, know it all, guests will arrive with more lessons to teach about human nature—theirs and yours. Serving breakfast, for example, should be an easy sort of task. One morning I was getting breakfast together while Hugo went out for eggs. When he came back, jazz was playing in the dining room, coffee was brewing, and I was taking hot biscuits from the oven. Green tomatoes, coated with cornmeal, were fried and in the warming oven, ham browned on the stove. The breakfast these guests requested was coming together nicely.

"What happened?" he said, walking in the kitchen door.

"What do you mean?"

"Guests are gone."

"They can't be."

"Look for yourself. The front door is wide open and their car is missing."

Half an hour later when they still weren't back, we went up to check their room. The key lay on the dresser, their luggage was gone.

We ate their breakfast in gloomy silence. Because they'd paid in advance, we didn't come up short, but the experience led to a sign, a small act of defiance, in the front hall:

PLEASE CLOSE DOOR
SO COYOTES DON'T GET IN!

• • •

There are many philosophies about what makes a person. You are what you think. You are the work you do. You are what you love. You are where you live. You are what you read, said François Mauriac, "but I'd know you better if you tell me what you reread." All partly right, but most completely right to my way of thinking is the biblical idea that you are what you give. Whatever we are able to give by way of comfort, good food, and a pleasing setting that I hope leaves space for the imagination, the souls of the guests, it has all come back. Beyond the gifts, the wine, crab cakes, doorknobs, and so on—beyond that, more than a few guests leave behind something of themselves, a wise insight, a hard-won life lesson, a way of being.

Bad things happen, I know it. Why, after all, should we be any different from anyone else? I know it from the stories other innkeepers tell about the strain on their personal lives and relationships, and about trying guests. The guest who ironed on an antique table and left a deep burn. The guests who ate pizza in bed, ruining the duvet. The guests who lit hundreds of candles and almost burned down the house. The guests who held a "small wedding party" that started with warming up a whole roasted pig in the fireplace and ended with beer cans and meat bones strewn around the floors alongside the sleeping guests.

Another time a woman I didn't know leaned across the table at a dinner party on hearing our plans to open a B&B and said, "Oh, you'll just hate it. My mother had one for a few weeks, until she saw guests on the way out to their car, carrying boxes packed full of furnishings from the room they stayed in, pictures in frames and everything. Kleptos are a big problem at B&Bs."

A friend tells about his brother's bed-and-breakfast, a main house and cabins in Montana. A group that turned out to be Hells Angels reserved the cabins. When the partying got wild and they started destroying the place, the police were called. A death threat was issued against his brother, who now prefers to spend his time in Mexico.

But my favorite cautionary tale is not so much about bad guests as it is about Innkeeper's Mistake Number One. After a couple departed, leaving behind an expensive nightgown, this host called up the guest to ask if he should mail it. The wife, who answered, knew nothing about a weekend away and the host and husband in question narrowly escaped lawsuits. Not one to make the same mistake twice, this host was thriving last I stayed at his place. We compared notes. He, like us, has a drawer full of left-behind paraphernalia. Ours is heavy on reading glasses, pens, and . . . negligees. Three of these, each lacier and more provocative than the one before, hang on Hugo's closet door, one green, one white, one black. Why?

I think they're kind of interesting, he explains.

I wait for the truly dreadful thing to happen and when it does I only hope to be ready, able of mind and body, to deal with what may come, grateful that, whatever it is, it didn't happen at the very beginning when we desperately wanted to please everyone and be liked. Of course I also realize and appreciate that in this particular place we exist under a protective aura. A nineteenth-century parsonage in the countryside self-selects a certain kind of guest.

So it's a joy when guests arrive and it's a joy when they leave. When checkout time comes, the room keys are back on the desk in the hall, the last car crunches on the driveway gravel, the last good-bye is waved, and the money is in your pocket—then the clock can be stopped for an hour, maybe longer if no new guests are arriving. On a Sunday morning, two servings of breakfast pudding are set aside and by noon we sit down on the porch or in the garden, guests for an hour in our own place.

If all the guests are out on a Saturday night, we might walk out on the grass and do a few steps to music coming from a party at the inn across the road or wander into the back field, which in May turns to a mirage of limpid yellow light, thousands and thousands of buttercups. The most surprising of gifts, the yellow stretches as far as you can see, all the way to a line of cedars and oaks at the horizon. I make a mental note to ask the farmer who tills this land what makes the buttercups bloom each spring before he plants corn or soybeans.

The burnout rate in this business is high. Most who start out full of energy, optimism, and enthusiasm have had enough and are gone in seven years. Those who stay after the seven-year mark stay a very long time. I don't know which we will be, but for now I know that if you like people and work, can set up a place that lets both the guests and the hosts feel comfortable in very separate quarters, if your business plan and, not least of all, your working partnership are solid, and all the other ifs—it can sometimes be heaven.

A Curious Ballast

BACK IN MY OTHER LIFE, CHANGE WAS LONG OVERDUE. It wasn't the politics or competitive culture of the museum where I worked at the time and it certainly wasn't the work itself that got to me. I loved editing art books that lived long lives in scholarly libraries and museums, loved producing them on fine paper with beautiful endsheets, full-color reproductions, and sewn bindings. It was a real privilege to participate in the making of these books.

No, after a dozen years it was the inexplicable, blinding headaches that set in whenever I went to the office. I became obsessed with the idea that in the throes of one of these "ice-pick" headaches, a monstrous mistake would strike, not only humiliating me but, far worse, the museum.

The gods of publishing had been kind for a good, long time and I worried how much longer it could last. In a typical three-hundred-page book of a hundred thousand words in three or four languages with five hundred images, the probability of an error had to be high. No matter how carefully I checked proofs, it was always an act of faith to sign off and print. I kept a sheet of blue paper in my top desk drawer, a gift from another colleague when I first arrived at the museum, a constant reminder to be careful. Handwritten in blue ink, it read:

The Six Phases of a Project

1. Enthusiasm
2. Disillusionment
3. Panic
4. Search for the Guilty
5. Punishment of the Weak
6. Praise & Honors for the Nonparticipants

That, and a story told by a renowned art historian when we met to discuss the editing of his book, kept me on continuous high alert. Working with another editor, the art historian said quietly, an appalling error occurred. The historian himself approved the text and verified the placement of every image. In the middle of the night, the printer phoned the editor because one image was incorrectly oriented: You could clearly see the upside-down signature of Michelangelo. The editor approved rotating the image and the presses rolled.

The book was printed and bound. Unfortunately, the drawing in question, the subject of the volume, was now upside down because Michelangelo often used a sheet of valuable paper more than once, turning it around to sketch his flow of ideas. The art historian peered at me over the tops of his half-frame glasses: We can't be too careful, can we?

In the bend of his head, his eyes lowered as if fending off invisible blows, you could see that Hugo was more disillusioned than I was. His store, The Bookstall, a community fixture and gathering place for nineteen years just outside Washington, D.C., went the way of hundreds of other independents when the chain booksellers with their extraordinary selection of titles entered the picture.

When it closed, the store left him with a lot of debt and fond memories of the book lovers who came to browse, shop, and exchange news. Among the celebrity customers there was one who liked to shop in his pajamas. Every Christmas Eve a car let him off at the door and he sat in the Bookstall's back office while Hugo made recommendations, brought him books to peruse and discuss before wrapping up his selections. With a fountain pen from his bathrobe pocket the customer wrote out gift cards. The staff did their best with Hugo preoccupied for two hours on the busiest day of the year, but it wouldn't have been Christmas without this interlude.

For a broadcast journalist, Hugo always kept copies of the *Meditations of Marcus Aurelius* in stock because this one customer, Ted Koppel, liked to present the small volume of Stoic wisdom as a gift when he interviewed heads of state. Hugo stacked the *Meditations* on a shelf right inside the front door because Koppel was always in a hurry. One day Hugo asked him what part of the *Meditations* he himself was most drawn to. Right here, Koppel opened to a page: "Accustom yourself to reflect upon the universality of change." Just an ordinary day at the bookstore.

Another time, Linda Pastan brought in a poem titled "The Bookstall" that she had written about her experience in the shop, later published in a collection of her work:

Just looking at them
I grow greedy, as if they were
freshly baked loaves
waiting on their shelves
to be broken open—that one
and that—and I make my choice
in a mood of exalted luck,
browsing among them
like a cow in sweetest pasture.

For life is continuous
as long as they wait
to be read—these inked paths
opening into the future, page
after page, every book
its own receding horizon.
And I hold them, one in each hand,
a curious ballast weighting me
here to the earth.

The bookstore brought in John McPhee to sign copies of his latest book. It brought mystery writers Tony Hillerman and Martha Grimes. Books brought Hugo face-to-face with John Ashbery, Helen Frankenthaler, Ansel Adams, James Dickey, and Arthur Ashe. Most thrilling in the view of my daughters, Lucy and Amanda, who worked in the store when they needed money, was seeing Wonder Woman, actress Lynda Carter, shopping for books for her children. Lucy, just turned twelve, volunteered to work for free on Saturdays when Wonder Woman liked to shop.

Hugo's own personal favorites were the families who came, bought, read and discussed books, and brought their children along year after year to share the experience. These regulars became good friends who had a way of turning up later, in our new life, to repay his favors. Hugo helped their children start with *Goodnight, Moon* and go on through E. B. White to Stephen Crane and Edith Wharton in their high school years. When these children returned to work in the bookstore and pointed out books they'd enjoyed to new young customers, the bookstore family circle was complete. Books and a small store that the neighborhood treated like their own living room. It seemed like a dream.

Falling back on his other great interest, Hugo tried cooking next. Being Italian, he passionately loved food, cooking, and eating. A good idea, I thought. Work and love, Freud said after all, are the most important parts of a life.

Cooking school proved as pleasant as the images created on TV by celebrity chefs. But the restaurant kitchens where he worked after training were nightmares straight out of George Orwell. At a lovely pastoral restaurant favored by Washington A-list types, Hugo started out as a line cook and in the second week did his first turn at "Fam," the family-style meal cooked for staff each afternoon before opening for business. The rule was to use up whatever was left, and so Hugo turned out a Bolognese sauce with rigatoni. Later in the evening as the restaurant was closing down, a senior waiter found Hugo alone by the grill and hissed: "If you ever cook Italian for us again, I kill you." A catering company where Hugo could be the boss seemed like a better idea.

The trouble was that his interactions with others in the aptly named profession of catering did not live up to the life of the bookstore. Once he discussed William Styron, Julia Child, and the *Rubaiyat of Omar Khayyam* all in a morning's work. Now he was summoned to palatial homes to prepare, on one occasion, risotto the way the client had it in Rome, with no specifics available. When the risotto, lacking saffron, didn't meet the client's expectation, it was sent back and Hugo was called into the dining room to discuss it before the assembled dinner party. When he was hired to prepare a buffet for seventy-five people but a hundred turned up and the food ran out, the client was furious.

Hugo decided to find a different way to make a living.

At a historic summer camp on Martha's Vineyard, he did a stint as chef, preparing breakfast, lunch, and dinner for ten to forty guests a day. He was in charge of the kitchen, which came complete with "chore girls," as the summer helpers were called, who chopped vegetables, made sandwiches, and washed the kitchen dishes. The "chore boy" helped Hugo carry the food up to the dining room in an old barn.

To keep the chore girls' spirits up, Hugo let them make desserts, which they turned out with enthusiasm. This saved Hugo time and the chocolate mud pies, chocolate mousse, and double-chocolate brownies did wonders for everyone's morale. Hugo began to think that we would both move there full-time the second year. My role wasn't exactly defined, but I would help out and get to do some of the interesting cooking. The office headaches were getting worse and I cut back to four days a week, taking unpaid medical leave.

A true dream job, everyone who heard about the camp said, and the cachet of the setting drew friends who came and worked in the kitchen for free, just to be there, just to experience it. The camp, on a hilltop, overlooked vistas of old stone walls and green fields, complete with grazing sheep, stretching down to Chilmark Pond and the Atlantic Ocean beyond. Since 1919, artists, writers, and liberal intellectuals gathered there to relax, work, exchange ideas, and frolic, which included nude swimming at the secluded beach. Over the years members included Thomas Hart Benton and Max Eastman.

It was only a matter of weeks until Hugo discovered what was wrong with this dream. First, there was the Lobster Lady. Every week after lobster night, she collected the carcasses from all the dinner plates as she had been doing for as long as anyone could remember, maybe fifty years. Then she sat in the barn doorway for hours extracting any remaining shreds of meat from the shells and mixing it up with mayonnaise. After that it went into an ancient refrigerator. The next evening she served it on crackers to the guests.

She offered a lobster canapé to Hugo. He politely declined, but she set one on the kitchen counter where he was working. "Waste not, want not," she said and headed off to the dining room with her tray.

"Do you have any idea how many rules of sanitation that violates?" he whispered to me from the only working phone on the property. "People have *chewed* on those shells—the bacteria! The lobsters shouldn't be re-refrigerated after all those hours out in the heat, the mayo is a perfect medium for a sanitation disaster and if anyone gets sick around here they'll blame me." No one got sick, but Hugo said it was only a question of time.

The second problem, also a sanitation issue, was the milk. Custom dictated that milk be served in its bottles on the tables to adults and children alike. Leftover milk was put away for the next meal. In the heat of summer Hugo recognized this as a poor idea. He poured the milk into pitchers and discarded any unused milk after each meal. The main supply remained relatively safe in the fridge. He was reprimanded.

He persisted and a meeting was called. Hugo was ordered to reinstate the milk bottles on the tables.

Third, and worst, his living quarters, a picturesque cottage on the hillside above the camp, had no shower or toilet. Those were communal and located a quarter-mile away. In addition, when he left the kitchen at night to trek back through the thick woods to the cottage, he needed an Army-issue mosquito helmet. This exquisite setting also happened to be an epicenter of Lyme disease. When I visited to preview our new life, the tick bite and rash I got took six months to clear up.

Back to the drawing boards. Hugo read and reread Paul Hawken's books and listened to his tapes. Work should be play, he repeated like a mantra; play should be your work. An almost impossible dream for most of the world, but if you've ever experienced it, ever come close, the concept is always out there, beckoning, tempting you. Hugo missed the daily flow of people, books, and ideas, the sense of place and community that were a good bookshop. We took a short vacation to a bed-and-breakfast to regroup and think.

Hugo observed the owner of this bed-and-breakfast on Martha's Vineyard, who happened to be Hugh Taylor, brother of James Taylor, emerging from the kitchen in an apron to greet guests, then outside repairing bicycles in the shade of an old tree or bringing in baskets of fresh produce. Later he saw Hugh and his wife Jeannie, who seemed to enjoy working together each in their separate spheres during the day, then deep in conversation with guests as they presided over happy hour.

We looked around at the other guests at this bed-and-breakfast. With few exceptions such places seemed to attract nice, interesting, bright people. Good food, books, conversation, and music with people who are on vacation and likely to be in a pleasant frame of mind—it looked like a solution worth gambling on.

It was easy enough to say, but facing up to the risks caused sleepless nights for months. How do you justify ditching everything you know, and have some experience—even proficiency—at, for the new and uncertain? Questions from friends, colleagues, and family hinted politely at this. Only the oldest of my children, Ethan, dared a blunt joke: "A business plan by a red-ink bookstore owner and an editor—great. Maybe you can think up a tax-deductible business for me, too." We stood to lose much more than pride if the new idea didn't pan out. Hugo was still paying off bookstore debt and more debt on top of it would sink our boat.

Assuming we found a fixer-upper house and were able to transform it into an appealing bed-and-breakfast, if real estate prices fell or if the bed-and-breakfast failed to attract enough business, we would be in a sorry state. At the office when I hired editorial help, there were always stacks of resumes for every position and at higher levels the competition was fierce, with directors of other publishing programs applying to work with the rank and file in ours. If I left, I would never get my job back, or one close to it.

The rational mind urged staying put, trying to keep doing what you've always done well. Forget about reinventing, redefining, retooling, reengineering. Forget taking a leap of faith and striking out in a new direction.

This is what almost everyone we know—friends and family alike, in professions from medicine to law to teaching to business—has done. This they judged to be the wise course. The only three exceptions, who did not stay put because they lost their jobs or quit, were worth noting. Two went on to make a spectacular success of redefinition; the third, who went into day-trading, crashed and burned the first time the stock market took a dive.

My own sister, a bank director, survived mergers and take-overs for decades. When the latest round of new young bosses arrived, she sensed that her days were numbered. The bank wanted its executives young and lean and actually warned them about gaining weight. She was as lean as anyone, but she couldn't help getting older. A music major back in college, she had set her flute aside to earn a living. Now she dusted it off and began practicing. She started flute lessons again. She organized a trio. When the ax fell, her trio already had book-ings. She trained as a Suzuki flute instructor and went on to a full schedule of teaching and performing.

From getting down on the floor, eye to eye with her youngest students, coaxing them to make a beautiful sound for their favorite teddy bear, to attending advanced training sessions with the master teachers and musicians, to performing with her trio and other ensembles, it's a rosy picture. The only shadow is the competition for a coveted position with an orchestra. "I'm doing as well as I can, but I'm competing with musicians who have played the flute two hours a day for thirty years. That's a little disappointing. No matter how hard I work, I'll never make up for that."

The second eye-popping success was a close friend I'd known since our sons were born, who worked as a lawyer for the federal government. Deciding that she had accomplished as much as she could there, Rita landed a plum university position when she "retired" that allowed her to conduct research, teach, write, and promote racial diversity. This opportunity, like my sister's, did not fall from the sky. Before entering law school, this friend had initiated a class action suit against the state of Tennessee for a system of higher education that discriminated against African Americans. "If I had known more at the time, I probably wouldn't have tried it," she said when the case was finally settled thirty-eight years later, bringing her public attention and the new job. She sees this as the third and final phase of a career devoted to public service and equality issues.

Several acquaintances have made less dramatic changes with mixed results: boredom and a sense of unease at consulting in their fields, rather than being at the center of their universes. But everyone else we know is staying put, doing what they've always done well, a careful and evidently contented group.

One reason our plans raised eyebrows had to do with the "service industry" aspect of the new business. "Do you think

Carol has the . . . stamina for all the bed-changing and clean-ing?" my sister asked Hugo in confidence. "I hope you'll enjoy the innkeeper's tasks," a museum colleague remarked. "Lotsa luck," said Hugo's brother Paul, a neurologist. The remarks jolted me, but only momentarily, because I chose to dwell on the creative aspects of our plans, rather than the mundane ones.

Another reason was that we weren't exactly forced into change, though it wasn't exactly voluntary either, which made it harder for friends and family to understand and support. Either way, I saw the same questions waiting for us down the road: Does it work? Have you moved in an exciting, coura-geous, and sustaining direction—or not?

Not being a superstar lawyer or a banker–turned–flutist, or one of the wunderkinds you read about who retires from a lucrative corporate job to start a foundation for the arts or another good cause, Hugo and I were hoping for a modest transition. But would we land on our feet, be able to pay our bills, provide a respite for others, and be a little happier our-selves? It all sounded too uncertain, too risky.

On the other hand, Hugo argued, and I had to admit the point, how many more years will go by before it's too late? If you don't have the stamina for change now, do you think you'll have more when you're older? The current path, though known, was one neither of us wanted to continue down. I didn't try to assess the odds of failing. The uncertain-ty was undeniable, but this could be a last chance at building a life that would take not just one or the other of us, but both, somewhere better. Every silver lining has clouds, I reasoned. At least they will be new clouds.

Hugo prowled country roads extending out from Washington for two years—long, tiring trips that always ended in no prospects—before he came across a last chance kind of place.

Royal Oak

THREE STORIES HIGH, WITH EIGHT HUGE WINDOWS ON the first floor alone, seven more above, the house's steep cross gables each sheltered a small, arched window in which you could almost see a rocking chair and lace curtains. Stately, it had presence in a shaky sort of way.

Hugo had driven up and down the Bay Hundred peninsula from St. Michaels to Tilghman Island all day, exploring back roads down to the water, looking for properties for sale. Calling it quits, he headed for home and happened on an out-of-the-way village we had passed through once on a bicycle trip. He was curiously fond of the place, but neither of us could have pinpointed it on any map.

Now a decade or two later, he stopped in front of a rusted iron gate with a "For Sale by Owner" sign. "I felt like I was in a cheesy movie," he told me that night. "The house is actually ... perfect. An angular, white Victorian, a cozy grandmother's house. It looks like a bed-and-breakfast."

This was not a turreted Queen Anne Victorian, laden with gingerbread, but a true country Victorian, decorous, yet with touches of trim in the simply curved decorative brackets on the porch and delicate cut-out pattern above the bay windows, like the veil on a lady's hat. A stand of tall maples clustered to one side of the deep, shady yard, and a long weedy driveway led past the south side of the house and porch to a pleasing outbuilding, maybe once a barn, with massive, painted wooden doors. Directly across the country road was an imposing waterfront inn, graciously standing ever since the 1700s and now with a putting green, too. Hugo thought that no mini-mart or gas station would ever be built there in our lifetime.

Maybe it would be a safe investment and provide the life we pictured, running an elegant bed-and-breakfast, living happily ever after. "Of course there's still some work to be done," he said that night as we sat up late talking. "All within my ability, though." Yes, a couple of windows were boarded up and a rusted propane tank occupied a prominent position near the front door, but that could easily be moved. He pulled a paper napkin out of his shirt pocket on which he had scribbled a short to-do list:

> *Paint*
> *Landscape*
> *Cleaning*
> *Some carpentry?*

• • •

An off-the-map village of about a dozen nineteenth-century houses, a couple of shops offering used furniture and antiques, a gone-out-of-business church and parsonage, and a modern brick post office, all huddled together at the head of Oak Creek. That's the village of Royal Oak itself. Newer development dots the road on either side and spreads down innumerable fingers of land surrounded by water. The occasional unimposing gravel lane leads to a grand old plantation house at the water's edge. Something like this village might be found almost anywhere a confluence of geography and tradition has slowed the advance of mainstream development and culture. This particular village, two hundred miles south of New York City and ninety miles east of Washington, D.C., lies on Maryland's Eastern Shore, that is, not on the shores of the Atlantic Ocean but on the Chesapeake Bay, sixty miles to the west of the Atlantic beaches. It's clear if you've been there; clear as mud if not.

Royal Oak first attracted visitors about a hundred years ago to its inn, the Pasadena, which became a popular summer escape for residents of Washington, Baltimore, and Philadelphia. The new railroad and steamship service made it an easy trip. Then in the 1920s Gary Cooper and the entire film cast stayed at the Pasadena while making *The First Kiss*, one of his first starring roles, with Fay Wray. It was among the last of the lavish silent films, costing $200,000. Cooper played an oyster dredger who becomes a pirate to put his brothers through school and along the way falls in love with a wealthy tourist. The area's whole oyster dredging fleet—twenty-five skipjacks and bugeyes—was put under contract for the filming, which lasted six weeks. Another inn had refused to put up the film stars, fearing immorality, but at the Pasadena the stars earned respect for their hard work and quiet ways. For years afterward, young women came as summer visitors to the Pasadena, hoping to sleep in Gary Cooper's bed. According to one account, the wily innkeepers assured visitors that whatever bed happened to be available was the very one Cooper had slept in.

The village also began to enjoy a reputation for some of the best fried chicken around, and people were drawn by the aroma, it was said, from half a mile and more away.

Before all that came Indians, then trappers, followed by white land speculators and settlers. On vast plantations tobacco—sotweed—was grown and later, corn, wheat, and other grains. Slaves and indentured servants worked the land. Here, isolated from the mainland by water, insular ways thrived and persisted, for better, in the tightly knit communities of hardworking people, and for worse, in harsh racial divides. The fight for civil rights was especially bitter.

Although the international legal trade of slaves ended at the beginning of the nineteenth century, Maryland, along with Virginia, continued slave trading until the Civil War. As would be expected in a border state, Maryland harbored strong sentiments both for and against Emancipation. When the first Northern troops to respond to the call to arms arrived in Baltimore on the way to Washington, riots broke out. The governor of Maryland wired President Abraham Lincoln, saying, "The excitement is fearful . . . send no more troops here." Authorities then burned the railroad bridges linking Baltimore to the Northern cities.

The Eastern Shore was also home to two great abolitionists. Born into slavery, Frederick Douglass spent his childhood in Talbot County and started his work life as a slave at an estate near the town of St. Michaels. Judged to have an arrogant attitude, he was sent to the infamous "slave breaker," Edward Covey. Bearing permanent scars from whippings, Douglass escaped to the North to continue his lifelong pursuit of racial equality.

Harriet Tubman, born in the next county south, led many slaves north on foot, on the Underground Railroad, which passed through the region's woods, swamps, creeks, and rivers. After her own escape, Tubman returned at least nineteen times to lead hundreds of slaves to freedom, including her aged parents. Harriet Tubman was considered a saint by blacks and a devil by white slaveholders. The bounty placed on her head was $40,000. She was never caught, and as a "conductor" of the Underground Railroad, she said she "never lost a single passenger."

In and around the ports of the Chesapeake Bay, black ships' pilots helped fugitives and white boat captains also smuggled slaves north, sometimes for a bribe. Fleeing slaves traveled the bay so often it became known as Chesapeake Station.

After the war ended, animosity between pro- and antislavery factions of the Methodist Church continued. The Southern Methodists, who during the war were said to climb out the windows of a local church rather than walk under the American flag hanging over the doorway, were offended by the antislavery stance of the mother church. The Northern Methodists, equally critical of the Southern Methodists (citing as just one example the bishop who had refused to relinquish his wife's slaves), determined to establish a greater presence on the Eastern Shore, including an outpost in Royal Oak. In 1883 they constructed an imposing three-story parsonage, painted white with red sashes and green shutters, for a circuit-riding minister. The foundation was built of brick and solid oak timbers.

A few years later a fine white country church, complete with a graceful steeple and Gothic windows of pearlescent stained glass, was built close by. But the project did not flourish. The parsonage was sold off during the Depression and ten years later the church was abandoned.

By 2000 the church, painted ochre with turquoise trim, was home to an occasional business in used furniture. The roof leaked, siding had fallen away from the steeple, and some of the stained glass was cracked or missing. The parsonage, anchoring the other side of the village a quarter-mile away, retained shreds of white paint but was otherwise in similar dilapidated condition. Partly rented out and partly boarded up, this house that Hugo happened on, for sale by owner, had been on the market for seven years.

The owner returned our third phone call. He reminisced about happy childhood times spent at his grandmother's house, picking apples, hunting for arrowheads in the fields, and sliding down the steep, frontstairs banister while trying to hold a chamber pot upright. He refused to let the house fall into the wrong hands. Others had made offers, and he had turned them all down. He might sell it to us if we promised to restore it. It was a good house, he said, and a good location.

The tenants offered a different view of its location when we drove out to see the house together for the first time one Friday afternoon. "It's a real sweet house," the young woman who met us at the door said. "Of course, some people might be bothered by what goes on around here . . . smuggling, motorcycle gangs, too."

I glanced past her out to the yard and the garage. She followed my eyes. "They'll use the garage, nothing we can do about it. They just show up here late at night, fifty, sixty at a time . . ."

"I guess it gets pretty dark around here," I managed.

As she showed me around the first floor, I asked if she had any idea where these smugglers came from.

"Smugglers? They come in the Tred Avon River and they're up and down this road all night long. You know it's them because of how fast they drive. Sometimes they'll miss the curve and land in the ditch or they'll slam straight into the fence. That's how it got all dinged up."

At night she heard weird sounds coming from the padlocked and supposedly uninhabited second floor. "I don't know what could be going on up there." She gathered up her baby from the crib, held him close, and looked upward.

It was quite a performance, aimed at scaring us off, and more than once as she showed us around, Hugo and I exchanged knowing this-won't-work-after-all glances. Out in the yard the woman kicked at plastic sandwich bags, squished in the mud, which, she said, were a sure sign of drug use on the property.

Walking back through the house I saw an extensive computer setup next to the crib and a table covered with empty beer bottles and packages of sandwich bags. In the garage Hugo reported seeing bales of pink packing peanuts.

Whatever else, she was right about the house itself. Tucked away on a little-known byway, it was a sweet one or at least it had once been sweet. Set on high ground, its faded dignity was still evident in the churchlike windows and the formal, wrought-iron fence that ran across the front of the property. It felt like a place where we could reinvent ourselves.

It didn't look like a dangerous area, what with the country road, the small, neat houses, wide fields, and woods. Besides we were determined, Hugo and I.

Gossip about the neighborhood couldn't stop us. The house itself was clearly an authentic touchstone to history and, almost miraculously, the village retained an engaging aura of a bygone time. With a little more work than Hugo initially estimated on his napkin, we thought it could be a bed-and-breakfast.

Maybe more important, it was the only house to turn up in two years of hunting that we could almost afford. If we didn't act soon, the impetus for change, for remaking our lives, was going to drift away.

So the tenant could not put us off. Neither could the lawyer Hugo hired to make the deal happen. As we walked up the boxwood-lined brick path to his imposing office in Easton, the county seat, he had this to say:

"Royal Oak?"

Yes, I confirmed.

"The—boys are over there, you know."

He let the words linger. I did not know and it was going to be necessary to admit as much if I wanted more information.

"Really?"

"They're bad news," he confided. "Drunk, naked, firing shotguns at the moon, that type of thing."

We shook hands and I dismissed his remark just as I had dismissed what the tenant said. You can't believe everything you hear . . .

Or can you? The question would haunt me a hundred times in the next year, especially at night when I walked from room to room in this house, straining to see out windows, into dark corners, and up the unlit attic stairs, trying to discover the reason for a sudden clang or a window-rattling thump.

The owner, Robbie, had neglected the place for decades, but still regretted selling off his grandmother's house. So when our lowball offer insulted his family heritage, it took weeks of faxed apologies, many more promises that our intentions for the house were honorable, and, of course, more money to win his forgiveness. After that he dragged out negotiations for eleven months and put off two dates to close the deal.

On a return visit to Royal Oak, while we waited for him to set a third date, we found the tenants gone, but as we walked around looking the place up and down, a visitor arrived by bicycle.

Flying a red bandanna from his back pocket, Mr. Louis Scott Kilmon, in neat khakis, flannel shirt, and straw hat, dismounted inside the rusted iron fence, introduced himself, and offered words of welcome. He had heard we were buying the place. I said how much we liked the village.

He responded that he hoped it would stay that way.

He rested his hand on the fence. "A few years back, the feds came around here with big plans to widen the road." He waved at the narrow road following the creek that winds between our house and his, three doors down.

"Of course they didn't mention that right off. Tried to bribe us with promises of—" He paused and leaned into the words. "A *bike* path. So we told them we didn't want any fool bike path around here and we didn't want the road widened either. If they widened the road, then we'd really have traffic and there's too much already."

He shot an appraising look at Hugo and me.

One of my first thoughts about the area was that a bike or walking path would be a big improvement because the road has a three-foot drainage ditch on either side and no shoulders. But I decided not to say so right then. Obviously, there were other perspectives to be considered.

While I was thinking things over, Hugo spoke up. "I see what you mean."

"We don't want any bike paths around here," Mr. Kilmon repeated.

I decided our position on the spot. "We wouldn't want a bike path either."

Sensing our willingness to fit in, and undoubtedly wanting to keep a close eye on the newcomers, Mr. Kilmon would come by often once we took over the place some months later. Taking note of even tiny signs of progress, he always offered an encouraging word, which we lapped up like starving dogs. When the true extent of what we had to do to fix up the house before even starting a business began to dawn on us, and with it the constantly nagging thought that we were hopeless romantic fools, I looked to Scott's encouragement as validation of the project and the idea that it wasn't doomed.

He came to know as much about the project as we did.

"I see you're replacing those old cinderblock steps with mahogany," he might call out from his front porch as I walked by on my way to the post office.

"Yes, a gift from my brother," I called back on that occasion. He waved me over to his porch, from where he could conveniently observe all the comings and goings at the post office. It was the first invitation to sit on his porch so I quickly accepted, not suspecting what he had in mind.

I didn't want to overstay or seem impolite by leaving too soon and hoped half an hour was the proper amount of time for a first visit, country style. It was long enough for Scott Kilmon to extract most of my family history. His technique centered on the apparently casual, cunningly well-placed question. By asking if my parents were local, he got straight to the knowledge of my Maryland-born grandmother, which drew an approving nod, and the fact that my great-great-grandfather had preached to Union families at Antietam before the battle, which drew no comment.

After that, when walls and doors were down and renovation of the future bed-and-breakfast was in full swing, it was Scott who kept a close eye on the place.

"If you ever find anything missing, you just let me know," he said on one of his regular bicycle visits. "Between my brothers and myself," he added, "we pretty much see whatever's going on around here."

What Scott meant, I eventually found out, was that two of his brothers, a son, and a niece owned houses lining the main road into the village and also at the intersection of the second road, which leads to the little ferry, established back in 1683, to Oxford. (Further along, another road called Ferry Neck, by the way, does not go to the ferry.) This means that you can't easily enter or leave the village without being seen by at least one Kilmon.

It also explains why his niece feels comfortable closing up the used furniture and antiques shops at night just by draping rope across the outdoor displays of objects for sale.

In time I learned that Scott, a retired high school music teacher, is an environmentalist who heats his house with scrap lumber and that he is a gardener. Tourists will stop to photograph his artistic creation, the tomatoes on towering vines, the lettuces, lima beans, potatoes, squashes, spinach, cucumbers, okra, and peppers, all framed by red, orange, yellow, and magenta zinnias. In the background, sunflowers grow almost as high as his barn. Once one of our guests asked us if they might pick flowers from his garden. This would not be appreciated, Hugo advised. Scott's own Garden of Eden is what it is.

Scott's family settled in the area in the 1700s when much of the land was still forested. He himself never mentions this, I think because he belongs so intimately to this place that he doesn't feel any need to say it. I came across the information at the public library. Shipbuilding at the nearby ports of Oxford and St. Michaels first brought sea captains and merchants, shipwrights, lumberjacks, and blacksmiths, many as indentured servants, to the region in the seventeenth century. As trade picked up and shipping and shipbuilding prospered, more arrived and settlement spread out. By the 1750s, along

the only road leading down the peninsula to St. Michaels, sur-
veyors found a few old houses standing as the forerunner of the
village of Royal Oak along with "about forty apple trees." Over
the next century, a church, a general store, a carriage maker
and funeral director, a blacksmith, a schoolhouse, a post office,
and the nearby Royal Oak train station were established.

By the early 1900s "Black Cinders and Ashes," as passen-
gers called the Baltimore, Chesapeake and Atlantic Railway,
brought summertime visitors in substantial numbers to the
area. Spewing cinders and smoke, the train raced through the
countryside at more than fifty miles an hour. Others arrived
by steamship and carriages transported the vacationers down
shady roads to boardinghouses like the Pasadena, which
advertised for "summer boarders—$5 a week—children half
rates." The region began to promote itself as the "land of
pleasant living," "God's own country," and even "the healthi-
est place in America." In its heyday, Royal Oak boasted, in
addition to the post office and schoolhouse, two churches, two
saloons, one barbershop, and five stores.

Reserved about himself and his family's history, Scott
Kilmon easily shared his knowledge of the surroundings.

The gigantic white oak that, according to legend, gave
the village its name? "It stood just a few yards down from
my house in front of the general store."

Much has been written about this tree, and it is still discussed locally as if it had died recently. I was surprised to learn
that it has been gone for almost 150 years. Farmers banded
together under its branches to form the Hearts of Oak Company, which fought in the Revolution and then again in the
War of 1812. Forty feet around, it stood as a landmark for at

least two centuries and it must have been quite a sight, to judge by a local historian's description of the tree "majestically clad in his forest green, a king in the forest, truly a Royal Oak."

At one point the tree was trimmed back because, according to a news account, "the branches overspread the county road, causing a menace to travel." When the tree finally died, it was widely lamented:

> In the passage of time all things must decay—as an evidence of this, the Old Royal Oak, about eight miles from Easton, so extensively known since the Revolution, and more recently since the War of 1812, from being pierced in both conflicts by the balls of some of Britain's "Long Shooters," and ever since having some of them suspended from its limbs—has from old age and the heat of the summer's sun withered and died. This old tree has a tremendous body and no one living, we presume can tell its age.
>
> *Easton Gazette*, July 31, 1868

A competing story about how the village got its name centers on the shelling of the town of St. Michaels, three miles away, during the War of 1812. Known as "the town that fooled the British," St. Michaels would have suffered considerably, according to the locally published history, *Tales of Old Maryland*, but for "the long head of one General Benson" who ordered the houses darkened and instructed residents to carry lights to their upper rooms and roofs. This, it was said, caused the British on ships in the harbor to aim their cannonfire too high and largely miss St. Michaels. Two shots did reach the huge oak tree over in Royal Oak, according to this version of events, which was thereafter called the Royal Oak. While Benson can certainly be credited for preparation of the town's defense, Pete Lesher of the Chesapeake Bay Maritime Museum observes, "The lantern story first appeared in print in the *Tales*, almost a century after the battle, and contemporary sources make no mention of lanterns or a blackout."

In any case, two cannonballs with metal straps crafted by a Kilmon ancestor hung for many years in the Royal Oak. Did they really come from a British ship? I asked Scott.

"Probably not," he thought. "More likely, militiamen brought them back as a souvenir, but they did hang there in the tree for years and periodically it was sport for someone to steal them."

Whoever stole the cannonballs always returned them, he said. "So now we keep them locked up in the post office."

This is true. You can see them suspended from the ceiling over a display of postal service envelopes. Near the cannonballs hangs a framed, yellowed newspaper clipping about the famous Royal Oak fried chicken, which visitors enjoyed at the inn, along with the fresh air, sandy beaches, boating, fishing and crabbing, "watermelon feeds," dancing to live band music, and relaxing in hammocks strung in "cozy nooks" among the trees.

How to make this famous fried chicken turned out to be one of those secrets folks were not in a hurry to share. The postmistress, Miss Ebbie, answered vaguely. Someone else suggested asking the man who helped Hugo haul away a lot of junk from our property, whose family has lived in the area for generations. If members of his family hadn't been cooks at the Pasadena, they would know someone who had cooked there. Hugo called him up to ask if I could come over. That's how things are done around here.

When I arrived fifteen minutes later, his sister uncovered a pan on the stove. "Is this what you're talking about?" I looked in the pan, which was full of crispy, caramel-colored fried chicken. Oh, yes.

After forking a serving onto a plate and handing it to me, she came to the point. "It's supposed to be made with lard, but you can do without."

While I ate, she gave me the recipe. "Buttermilk if you've got, to soak the chicken, then flour, salt, and pepper."

A few questions and answers later, I thought I had it.

It was easier finding out from Scott what happened to the general store that stood behind the Royal Oak Tree. Once filled with a vast array of dry goods, including ready-made clothing, boots, and shoes, along with groceries and medicines, it also offered favored turn-of-the-century souvenirs of a stay in the country: postcards, colorfully painted gourds, and dried sunflowers.

"The store was right here." Scott pointed to his front yard, filled now by the vegetable and flower garden.

"Needed sun for the garden, so my brother and I—"

He aimed another appraising look at the newcomers. *I know they're preservationists but are they rabid ones?* he was clearly thinking.

"So my brother and I—we *burnt* it down."

When the weather was nice, we visited back and forth in each other's yards and I came to know that Scott was always around and keeping an eye out. "Did you enjoy the evening last night in Royal Oak?" he asked at the post office early on a Saturday morning after I had arrived in town late the previous night.

Gradually, other members of the Kilmon clan emerged—Scott apparently served as their advance guard—and began to include us in village life so easily that I only noticed it long afterward. Scott's niece Julie let me bring furniture home from her shop to try out, to see if it fit, before paying anything.

Scott's brother Al had a stack of old green shutters for sale in his yard. I measured and thought that the shutters would fit the upstairs windows of our house. This was remarkable because all the windows had been individually hand-built and each one differs in size. Al sold the shutters for a song. When Hugo went to install them, he found that the hardware on the shutters matched the existing hardware on the house to the millimeter.

It shouldn't have been any surprise, when big trouble turned up in our second year, that our neighbors in Royal Oak came forward. Scott's wife, Susie, offered to help with anything at all. Julie's husband, Jerry, mowed the lawn. Other neighbors brought over venison and freshly caught rockfish.

Scott's son Steven brought a goose and someone else offered recipes. For children, cook a goose all day in a crock pot with a can of mushroom soup. For adults, braise a long time with orange, because the Canada geese that fly through here are tough birds.

And finally, at that time, came an invitation to hunt, which meant much, much more than it might seem. The importance of a local way, I came to understand, can be measured by how long it is withheld. The invitation to hunt was two years in coming.

Yes, there are hunting clubs around here and hunting guides. Yes, a limo will pull into the field behind our house, a hunter will get out, fire a shot, and return to the limo while the driver retrieves the dead goose and stows it in the trunk. This was different. This invitation to hunt with a neighbor meant initiation into one of the private worlds of the Eastern Shore, where people hunt for food to feed themselves and their families as they have for generations. Certain fields and farms are available at certain times—you have to know where to go.

But all that was later.

Robbie kept the third date we made to buy the property. At the lawyer's office, settlement on the house and the future direction of our lives took less than forty minutes.

Love and Remorse

A TANGLE OF VINES WOUND AROUND THE CHIMNEY and up into an old locust tree that leaned heavily against the front porch. The vines, poison ivy with leaves larger than a man's hand and a hefty trunk, were clearly succeeding in their plan to bring the locust down and the porch with it.

On the day of sale, the house looked much better than I'd remembered—taller, more graceful, and plainly once proud. Behind the overgrowth thirty feet high at the back of the property, lay a long, beautiful cornfield stretching to a line of trees at the horizon. At the same time it all looked much, much worse. How had I overlooked the leaning locust, four boarded up, broken windows, and seven "No Trespassing" signs? I could not picture it as someplace anyone would ever choose to visit—and pay for the privilege.

"Typical buyer's remorse," a friend later remarked, amused. "But I can't believe you fell for that old family heritage line."

On top of seller's and buyer's remorse, a third remorse hovered over the sale that morning, which the lawyer alluded to in few words. "The sheriff has taken care of things, I assume?" Robbie nodded and answered quietly. "Tenants are gone."

It was sad that the young mother and father who had tried to make a home in what was now our house had to leave. If not for us, I rationalized, then for someone else and no one could have predicted what happened to them. When their month-to-month lease was up, they refused to leave, so Robbie had to evict them and the sheriff kept watch while he carried all their possessions, clothes, furniture, baby toys, and new shoes—still in boxes—outside. People stopped by and picked over their things, neighbors said, until nothing was left. I wished I did not know that or that the family broke up. The mother went to her parents' house with the baby, people said, and the father, who stayed behind, landed in jail.

Knowing all this might have deterred Hugo or me alone, but together we were Bonnie and Clyde. The place had everything that makes old-house fiends swoon, from original wood floors to high ceilings to premodern air-conditioning in the form of windows opening to all four directions. It had original plaster and architectural detail, even a secret backstairs. The stairs were exactly like the steep, narrow backstairs at my grandmother's farmhouse where I loved to sit, eating her homemade caramels and eavesdropping on the grown-ups.

For Hugo, the house brought back memories of his childhood summer home. Both houses were a child's idyll and both were sold off when the next generation showed no interest in doing the work necessary to keep them up. The intersection of these two lost happy houses goes a long way to explaining our passion. It answered the large, pressing question that came to haunt Hugo as much as me: If not this house now, then what, and when? There was the money issue: You can't afford to be all that picky if you don't have much. Above all, the place suggestively promised the chance to fuse our pasts and future within its walls.

Squinting up at our new acquisition, our future, I tried to imagine lace curtains lifting in the bay breeze, a well-kept garden, guests strolling outside to admire the sun setting over the cornfield, Hugo and I holding hands and watching discreetly from the bay window. An appealing, old-fashioned flavor permeated the setting, yet it would be an easy reach for weekend visitors from Washington, Baltimore, Philadelphia, even New York. I reviewed our decision tree again and sighed. Buying an up and running bed-and-breakfast was out of the question.

It is easy enough to see slanted floors as quaint when anyone who knows anything, I had yet to learn, will see a clear red flag indicating structural damage. It was easy to dismiss what Hugo called "small collapsed areas" in the floors as he tried to minimize the problem. Once you fall into the rhythm of minimizing problems, it's easy, and if both partners agree to it, it's a cinch. After a while, you don't even have to think about it. An off-balance radiator ready to topple over and rip pipes from the walls? No problem. Ditto crumbling plaster which, more knowledgeable buyers will know, always waits until after a sale to start seriously falling. Ditto the cinderlike particles filtering out of faucets, the flaking lead paint on windowsills and doors, and the icing on our catastrophe, out in the utility shed, sinister gray dustings of asbestos. The home inspector had pointed out the asbestos to Hugo before the sale. Hugo didn't mention it to me until now because he didn't want me to worry.

The oil furnace, with long black pipes like giant spider legs, was another worry, but at least it worked. It had a *catch-pan* for dripping oil. Now those are words you don't want to hear if you have an oil furnace because it isn't supposed to need one. The pan, which I noticed but didn't mention because Hugo already looked concerned, brimmed with black oil. But even if I had understood what I was seeing before the sale, it wouldn't have made a difference. By now we were so attached to the idea of a bed-and-breakfast in this house, in this village, at this time that I saw no resemblance between this shaky structure and us.

Subliminally, though, I felt it.

When the nausea and exhaustion of full-blown buyer's remorse set in, I decided we should drive back to our house on the Western Shore, where I had lived much of my life, get some rest, even though we hadn't done anything except sit at a table to sign papers, and come back in a week or so to start work. Hugo quickly agreed and we headed for home.

It was more my home than Hugo's because I'd stayed on there after my marriage collapsed so as not to disrupt the children's lives any more than necessary. Eventually Hugo joined in there and helped raise the children. For twenty years he quietly wished for a home of our own. This was it.

In less than a minute, Hugo swung the truck around into a K-turn and headed back to the future bed-and-breakfast.

Pulling into the driveway again, we remarked that the evicted tenants still seemed to be gone. We discussed what to do, maybe look around some more. I climbed down from the truck and saw in the grass at my feet a man's hiking boot and small plastic baby toys, a red car, a green tree, and a blue block. I picked them up.

It was an icy, mouse-colored February dusk. There were few signs of life except for smoke puffs from a chimney down the road and the sound of the wind, punctuated by the distant spit of gunfire. The only bright objects in sight were new padlocks on the doors and the brilliant orange "No Trespassing" signs.

As Hugo leaned against the kitchen door to hunt for the key, the screws holding the padlock popped out of the rotting doorframe. The door swung open.

Trash and moldy rugs stretched in every direction. At least the furnace was running and it was pleasantly warm. I lined up the baby toys on the mantle, reached in my pocket for a red ribbon saved from Christmas, and went outside. Breaking a bough from the magnolia tree, I tied it up with a bow but the wind untied it so I settled for a knot. On the front door I found a rusty nail and hung it there, red tails flapping in the wind. I tore down two "No Trespassing" signs and stood back to see if it looked like someone lived here. Maybe.

Hugo came outside carrying our sleeping bags, unopened. He thought he'd see if the inn had a room for the night. The former Pasadena, now called The Oaks, was a busy place in season and he hoped it might provide some start-up business for us when they were fully booked. I never imagined being grateful for it so soon.

As we registered at the inn, I reminded Hugo as much as myself that we could not make a habit out of this even though the manager gave us a discount, clearly out of pity. You could see it in her eyes.

The idea of a warm, clean, comfortable bed for the night lifted my mood and I went back to the house to start cleaning. Upstairs I surveyed the filthy rooms and the radiators laced with cobwebs. I like radiators, with their gentle warmth, soothing hiss, and all-around handiness for warming up pajamas and snacks. My sister and I knew that on a cold night with the heat turned up, the marshmallows and chocolate for s'mores set on top of a radiator would melt in the time it took to change for bed.

Since we couldn't afford to replace these radiators, I got to work. As a child I learned how to clean radiators from my mother, who believed it built character. To do this, you take a long, narrow brush in one hand, the hose attachment of the vacuum cleaner in the other, hold your breath, and brush between the pipes while sucking up the dust. The second step is to wipe all the radiator's horizontal and vertical surfaces with disinfectant.

Character-building, maybe. A bigger benefit came from telling my own children about radiators and radiator cleaning in hopes of getting some help around the house.

Downstairs I heard Hugo ripping up carpeting.

"This really isn't so bad," I called to him as we passed on the stairs or in the hall. "It will be fine," he answered as he lugged junk out of the house, everything from leftover food to old rugs, to a desiccated animal. He held it up by the tail.

"It's an r-a-t!"

"Not necessarily," he said. "It *could* have been a squirrel. But even if it was an r-a-t, it's been dead a long time."

"How long?" I was thinking about how much a second night at the inn would cost and if they might give a discount again.

"Come take a look at it."

I stood in the doorway. "I can see fine from here. How long do you think it's been dead?"

"A very long time."

Hugo usually knows when to change a subject. "Honey, look at the bright side. In six months, with a little carpentry, a little paint, we'll have this place up and ready to go. You can decorate, arrange flowers. There will be guests. Let's open champagne tonight."

The next day my sister, in Washington on business, drove out to see for herself how much trouble Hugo and I had gotten into. She left the car engine running, came in, took a quick look around. In less than five minutes she was ready to leave. She's known for speaking her mind, so I didn't have to wonder what she really thought.

"I don't need to go upstairs," she said. "I get the idea."

I stood in the driveway and waved good-bye, thinking how much I would have given for a word of encouragement.

That night I fell asleep in a haze of self-pity. In the morning I woke up to the heart-stopping sound of gunfire.

Hugo lay motionless next to me in his sleeping bag. Are we being attacked? I whispered.

He turned over. "Why not relax where you are, stay away from the windows?" It was the ultracool voice he uses when something is really wrong. "I'll check it out."

Getting up, he edged along the wall to the window and looked out.

The gunfire stopped at that instant, then started up louder than before.

"I guess the neighbors don't like us. They don't want any outsiders—come-heres, I think they say."

"No, that's not it. They're firing away from the house, about fifty yards off. It just sounds close. That was a rifle, a twenty-two . . . Now they've moved on to a twelve-gauge shotgun."

After another silence there was more shooting.

Now Hugo didn't sound calm. "That's a two-twenty-three."

"What's that?" I zipped up my sleeping bag.

"It's what you'd use to take down a lion."

Next he identified a forty-four magnum going off, and after that a semiautomatic forty-five.

"Jesus! Someone around here has a lot of firepower."

A barrage started that sounded like the finale in a gangster flick. Hugo flattened his body against the wall and moved away from the window.

"What's *that*?"

"That is an automatic assault weapon."

I thought about the former tenants. "Drug dealers?"

"Who knows? Maybe we'll work inside today."

It got very quiet. Hugo went downstairs to make coffee

and when the reassuring dark-roast aroma drifted up to the bedroom, I climbed out of my sleeping bag and went down. Sitting on the floor away from the windows, we drank coffee and planned the day's projects. When it had been quiet for half an hour, Hugo decided to go out and look around. He came back, saying he did not find any bullet holes or broken glass around the house. If it stayed quiet, he thought we could go outside later.

That afternoon when Scott Kilmon biked by, Hugo flagged him down. We stood in the driveway talking weather until Hugo got around to saying, the way males do when they need information but don't want to be caught asking for it, "Some gunfire this morning."

Scott nodded. "Yep."

"Trouble around here?"

"Probably not."

"Well, that's good."

Scott was playing the game. Humiliating himself, Hugo finally got out an actual question.

"You hear anything over at your place?"

"Heard a couple of rounds," Scott said. Then he looked at Hugo.

"Probably the deputy sheriff. Lives a few doors up from you."

"And?" I tried to help out.

"Sometimes on weekends he target shoots."

Hugo had not fired a gun since high school, when he joined the rifle club out of a vague sense of self-preservation. Once his parents decided this was not an optimal educational environment, he landed in a military boarding school where he also figured that being on the rifle team might be a safe bet for a new kid. Although he qualified as an expert marksman, he never liked guns and after high school his rifle stayed in the closet.

When Scott left, Hugo said he might get his gun cleaned.

This struck me as a bad idea. We were supposed to be creating a tranquil bed-and-breakfast experience for guests from the cities seeking rest and relaxation, I pointed out, not a rod and gun club. Hugo said nothing, which meant he was planning to ignore my advice.

Frankly?

THE NEXT WEEKEND, LOADED WITH OPTIMISM, HUGO
packed saws, lumber, sandpaper, and scrapers into the back
of the truck and I added a dozen paint and fabric samples, a
vase, and a clock. Time to stop dreaming, time to work.

Pushing open the unlocked side door of the future bed-
and-breakfast, I sensed something wrong, though I couldn't
immediately say what it was.

A wave of cold hit my face as I stepped inside. It was
cold in the kitchen, in the sunny dining room, the parlor, and
upstairs—a deep, biting cold. I checked the thermostat. Forty
degrees. In the hall I noticed the corner of a white envelope
under the front door. Our first mail in the new house, probably

a note of welcome from a neighbor, I thought, forgetting the cold for the minute, maybe even an invitation. I ripped it open. A season's greetings card from the local oil company.

Hugo took the card out to the field behind the house where cell phones sometimes worked, and called them up. Wind whipped across the field to the side porch where I waited. After sunset it would get colder. We could work in parkas, but with the prediction of a hard freeze coming, the pipes were in danger.

Less than half an hour later the oil company man knelt in front of the furnace. A dark, foamy excrescence oozed from a pipe. "Doesn't look good."

"Did it die?" Hugo asked. I knew from his studied calm that we were both thinking the same thing. A big unexpected expense.

"Not that bad. Out of oil."

"But the owner said he would fill it enough for us to get started, or that's the first thing we would have done," I said, trying to pretend I wasn't a clueless come-here from the Western Shore.

"We would have filled it," Hugo said.

After wiping clean various parts of the furnace, he demonstrated how to ignite it. Then he went out to the yard and called on his cell phone for the oil truck, which arrived in less than ten minutes.

The oil tank filled, the furnace man turned the igniter. A groan came from a contraption behind him, an industrial-looking tank I hadn't noticed before. He jerked his head in the direction of this tank.

"Bet your water pressure's low, too."

At this point I decided to admit I didn't know anything

and just go for information. "How did you know that?"

"Water holding tank for your well keeps turning on. You need air in the top of the tank."

"How do you do that?"

The oil company man explained that all you have to do is turn a knob on the side of the tank, attach a hose, drain half the water out, then fill the top with air using a compressor attached on the opposite side.

"How much air?"

Depends on how much water you use, he said. We both thanked him and one of us mumbled something about old houses. He looked up then, taking his eyes off the furnace for the first time.

"Best thing to do with an old house? Take it as it comes."

He also explained how and why to bleed the radiators. As he got in his truck, he called out a final piece of advice. "Never can tell when someone who knows a house is empty might come by and siphon off your oil."

Hugo pulled the dangling, unused padlock off the side door and attached it to our new $500 oil supply.

Air *in* the water tank. Air *out* of the radiator so hot water can come in and warm the room. If only you could bleed the radiators and the tank would fill with air. By the time he left, the house had warmed up to sixty degrees and I unzipped my jacket, thinking about the former owner's choice of words. "Enough oil to get started."

"Frankly?" contractor number three said, echoing what the two before him had said less directly. "Knock it down and start over."

Hugo explained that we couldn't afford to do that. We needed to get a business up and running more or less right away.

"Better get a plumber then," he said on the way out.

Contractor number four looked around, admired the old woodwork, and stubbed out his cigarette on the dining room floor. "You've got a couple of foundation sills to replace, some floors... If you're not going to tear down, well, I'd say twenty-five thousand, maybe thirty, will go a long way toward fixing this thing up."

Repairing the listing foundation at the back of the house would run a fraction of that. He couldn't say exactly how much, but he'd only charge "time and materials, like all the contractors around here do with this type of job." I had heard about this local custom, and he came recommended. Elated that his estimate fit the budget, we hired him on the spot.

The correct order for doing the work, this contractor also explained, was foundation repairs first, then plumbing, then finishes. He couldn't count how many people got mixed up—he glanced at me—and started on finishes first, only to have to go back later and redo them.

Of course, we both said. I put away the color swatches and fabric samples I'd collected, the pretty magazine pictures of my ideal garden, and the catalogues of heirloom roses.

Hugo couldn't repair the foundation himself, but he intended to do the rest of the work, except for plumbing and wiring, with help from me when I wasn't at my day job. We sat up late making plans. Hugo drew up a bigger list now of everything we thought that needed doing.

1. Foundation: sound, according to home inspector,
except three sills and joists

2. Original wood floors in dining room, parlor, bedrooms,
owners' space: Keep and repair

3. Plumbing: Any pipes to replace? Furnace very old but
hopefully functional

4. Shed/laundry/furnace room: Fix or tear down and rebuild

5. Baths: One needed for each guest room

6. Kitchen: New appliances, sink, cabinets, flooring
(to replace linoleum), vent fan, lighting

7. Interior finishes: Patch and paint walls, ceilings,
doors (14), woodwork

8. Exterior: Siding and trim, scrape and paint

9. Front porch: Roof and foundation solid but some floor rot.
Build steps, balustrade, and cladding for spindly posts

10. Interior floor finishing: Sand all floors upstairs and down,
stain new wood to match original, seal

11. Landscaping: For curb appeal, work on front first—
take down dead tree, plant shrubbery along walkways,
around porch and driveway

12. Fences: Build high fence along side of property where
space "leaks" onto road. Paint antique iron fence and have
replacement sections made for gaps

13. Walkways: Replace concrete slab with old brick

14. Electrical work: Exterior lighting for walkways and ask
electrician to check entire house. Knob and tube wiring safe?

Each of these projects, we came to see, entailed another dozen or more associated tasks, some of which only emerged once you got into the project.

The general contractor turned out to be a fantastically lucky, if nerve-shattering break because he did exactly what he said he would do. He hired subcontractors, Larry and Buck, a father-and-son team who came to jack up the sagging sills, just three at the back of the house, and repair as many joists. They arrived promptly at seven every morning in a rusty, dented Camaro with the front seats replaced by aluminum lawn chairs tied down with bungee cords, and they sat together in the car having coffee and donuts before starting the dirty, dangerous work. Over the next days the slimmer of the two, Buck, in his old high school football jersey, slid under the house while his dad passed in shovels, concrete, jacks, bolts, and, last, new joists.

Hugo worried alternately that the house would collapse on them or that they would jack up the house so fast the remaining ceilings would come down. He ran outside the morning he heard Buck bellowing, "Daaaad, Daaaad!"

He found Buck wedged in tight under a joist except for one lower leg and hurried to get Larry, who was checking the jacks on the other side. Larry came around to where Buck lay, gave a powerful yank on his son's leg and Buck slid out uninjured, pants down to his ankles.

Maybe because of that, they jacked up the house so fast four windows popped their glass. An electrician who was upstairs at the time came running out screaming at them to stop because, "A mother of a crack is opening up in the back wall!"

That evening Hugo read that an old house should be jacked up very, very slowly over a period of days if not weeks so it can have time to adjust, stretch, and settle. A perfect description of what we needed in our own lives, but time and money were not going to allow. Even here some cracks were beginning to show. Hugo seemed disappointed that I couldn't spend more time on the project. I tried to fight off resentment that he had painted such a rosy picture of the work to be done.

The young carpenter who followed Buck and Larry came recommended by someone who couldn't fit the job into his schedule. Clear-eyed and articulate, this carpenter offered to frame up the new bathrooms for a reasonable fixed price, a necessary step before a plumber could come in. He could start right away.

The one and only existing bathroom upstairs first had to be gutted of its cheap, stained, and mostly broken fixturing. A former sitting room, it was spacious enough to divide into two baths, I realized, and situated, luckily, so that it would make en suite baths for two of the guest bedrooms. The sitting room for the third guest room had been turned into a kitchen by the former owner so the plumbing was already partly in place for a third bath.

Five days after the carpenter finished the better part of the framing, he vanished, leaving all his tools and materials neatly fanned out on the floor alongside a dead flying squirrel. I called him half a dozen times and left messages, offering to pay for what he had done, even if he couldn't complete the job. He never called back and in a month his phone was disconnected.

Something happened to that guy, Hugo kept saying, something bad. He didn't seem like the type to be spooked by the house's wildlife visitors.

Hugo studied the work, decided he could complete it, and did. It was a start. After that he went on to fit in about forty hours a week around the catering business he still ran to keep some money coming in. Eventually, he took down and put up walls, fixed doors, windows, plaster, and drywall. He patched, sanded, stained, and finished all the floors and trim—inside and out.

The problem was that the closer you looked at the house, the rougher you could see it was. It was easy to fall into self-loathing at our naïveté and there was a lot of time, while working, to consider exactly how we got into this pickle. Such feats of imagination are a survival mechanism, I decided, because they let you take leaps you would never otherwise consider.

Hugo didn't start out knowing how to do this work, but he learned fast. There was no choice. We needed to open for business before money ran out. By night he read up on home repair and watched a lot of episodes of *This Old House* on TV. By day he decided to work alongside a handyman for a month, someone who would let him watch and help. He needed to learn skills, what tools to buy, where you could take a shortcut, where you couldn't. The carpenter's work, even without the carpenter himself, had taught him some important basics.

Duane, the first handyman who returned our phone call, agreed to give Hugo a crash course in what he needed to know.

But at $18 an hour, eight hours a day, six days a week, we couldn't afford him for long. Duane also proved ingenious at linking one task to another so that he stayed on not for a month but two. At the end of his last day, we drank a beer together and he promised to come back anytime we got stuck.

My eyes welled up as his dented gray truck backed down the driveway. Now we were really alone with an enormous mess that looked, depending on time of day and blood sugar levels, almost impossible or completely impossible to fix.

Hugo eyed the gargantuan amount of thick drywall Duane had ordered, no doubt as job security for himself. Stacked three feet deep in the front hall, it instantly created a pitch in the old wood floor—something else to fix. Conveniently, this drywall, which wouldn't be needed for months, was so heavy Hugo couldn't possibly carry it up a ladder himself and hold it in place while nailing it to the studs. He called Duane.

Duane came back and helped with that, and then a day here, a week there. Every time we said good-byes, wished him well, and finished the day with a beer until it became a joke and we stopped saying good-bye.

A good work crew would have accomplished everything in six months. The miscalculation of how long it would take us was fourfold. To compensate, Hugo revved into high gear, working mostly alone five days a week, sometimes six or seven when there were no catering jobs. Time lost its usual meaning, speeding or slowing depending on how the work was going, but mostly it seemed nonexistent. In its place, strings of tasks stretched out of sight. While Hugo matched up doors he found in the garage with empty doorframes and got glass cut for all the broken and cracked windowpanes, I scraped away crumbled glazing, which holds panes of glass in old-fashioned windowframes, and learned to apply new glaze. This tedious process requires practice to create smooth, straight lines of glaze. My first attempts looked like fat, wiggly worms and because these were the prominent front porch windows, it all had to be chipped out and redone. I counted thirty-seven trips up and down the ladder before the first window was finished.

Taking a break from the physical work, I planned décor for the new bathrooms. Initially, I considered doing a vintage number with dark floors, wallpaper, and claw-footed tubs, then settled on an all-white, fully modern approach with a clean feel but with vintage touches, such as a vessel sink in one bathroom, a shell-shaped pedestal sink in another. A junk-store find—a mirror in a hand-carved frame with a flower motif and beautifully scraped clean of its paint to show pale wood—would hang Victorian-style from a molding on a dark blue, tasseled cord. Under a linoleum floor, Hugo discovered wide pine planks.

Whenever I took time to notice, the sun was always rising or setting. We dropped out, saw almost no one, and kept in touch with family mainly through late-night phone calls. Gatherings with friends, movies, books, dinner out, doctor checkups—all were set aside. Wisely, friends stayed away, even turning down invitations to stop by for a barbecue and check it out. "Thanks, we'll see it when it's done" was the unanimous response.

Family members took a different approach. Ethan, Lucy, and Amanda, along with my sister and brother, apparently discussed the situation among themselves and agreed it was serious, because they arrived at strategically spaced intervals, from Washington, Arizona, Michigan, Ohio, and New Jersey to encourage and lend a hand.

My sister announced that she didn't do home renovation. She would come to town and take us out to dinner. True to her word, Linda and her husband arrived a couple of months later, checked into an inn, and paid visits to the work site. One night we drove three miles into town to Paul Milne's restaurant. Feasting by candlelight on Paul's oysters in pink champagne sauce, local asparagus, filet, and good wine, with loving faces across the table, everything seemed possible. After eating, we sampled most of the restaurant's brandies. Each one brought more toasts for opening day and the success of our new life. I looked over at Hugo and realized how long it was since I'd seen him laugh. By the time we left, amused at everything and nothing, the project seemed wonderful again, even inspired. A burst of energy set in that lasted for months.

By some miracle my brother, the handiest, can-do member of the entire family, was on sabbatical that year from teaching and he came for two or three days at a time, sometimes a week, to work. Together Hugo and Rick installed a ninety-foot fence where the side of the property joined a public road. They tore down and rebuilt what was left of the front porch, built new windows, and every night they fortified themselves with pizzas, crab cakes, and beer. They drank more beer than I thought necessary, but Rick, a ceramic engineer, was studying the strength and "fracture behavior" of glass bottles for a lawsuit involving a beer company and he needed randomly selected empty bottles for testing, he explained as he unloaded four cases from the trunk of his car. I caught a flash of a grin.

"This is serious business, Carol," he intoned. "Do you think we should just pour all that good beer away?" Wastefulness, real or perceived, was a sin in our family to the extent that roasted chicken for dinner invariably meant creamed chicken the next night, and "shadow soup" the night after because the boiled bones by then left a shadow of taste. I shook my head. No one knows your flash points quite like a sibling. I went out to buy more ice for the beer.

The first of the children to show up, Ethan wanted to see for himself if the project looked like a reasonable investment or whether the time had come, I read in his face, for the grown children to start supervising their parents.

When he arrived one Saturday morning that first spring, he took his time looking around, and said carefully that he wasn't sure. Did we think paying guests would want to come here? Could we fix it up enough for that? He took off his jacket and offered to clear some of the overgrowth from the yard. He uprooted weeds, bushes, and massive vines around the ailing magnolia, which stands front and center as you approach the house. Magnolias don't like anything around their "feet," and someone had chopped off all this tree's lower branches and planted forsythia and Japanese honeysuckle there, so it was languishing. After Ethan finished clearing the area, he threw a shrugging glance up at its emaciated, lopsided, sixty-foot height and moved on to other parts of the yard. He worked with pitchfork, axes, shovels, and a chain saw, and I worked alongside him, talking about the economics of a bed-and-breakfast and about a house down the road that he might want to buy and fix up.

They were asking $25,000 for it. "Maybe we should get this place fixed up first," he said.

Hugo carried doors outside to scrape, patch, and paint and set up sawhorses near where Ethan and I were weeding and clearing more brush. Like my sister's visit, his made all seem possible, and good. By the time Ethan started putting away tools, the sun was low. I asked if he was hungry.

"Got to get going," he said.

I had understood he would stay for the night, having driven almost a hundred miles from Washington, and we would all have a pleasant supper together, made in the temporary kitchen Hugo set up in the driveway with an ice chest, grill, and garden hose. Ethan rattled his car keys.

"Got to get back to Washington," he said, looking up at the small third-floor window. "Been in the attic yet?"

Yes, why?

"I thought maybe I saw something up there . . . moving around." Ethan spent most of his time camping in tents on remote islands in the Indian Ocean or in underground bunkers on the North Korea border—the life of a computer consultant to the military. Practical, direct, efficient, he was not one to see ghosts and I thought he could have come up with a better excuse for leaving. Let it go, I thought as we hugged. Respect his time if you hope to see him again soon.

After he was gone, I called up Lucy and Amanda to tell them how much Ethan helped us, and how much fun we had. This brought Amanda down to the house two weeks later to help me scrape rust off the old iron fence, spray on rust preventive, and brush on shiny black paint. It was tedious going and the fence was 120 feet long. She asked how much she was expected to do. Grateful for the company, I assured her I never expected us to finish in a weekend. Can we go out to eat then? she asked. Go for a bicycle ride, maybe look in the stores?

The fence took me the rest of the spring, helped for a day here and there by Hugo, Rick, and Nancy, Ethan's wife. Nancy arrived during a late frigid blast and spent hours bundled in a knit hat, scarf, two coats, and gloves, scraping and painting. When the rest of us went inside for hot chocolate, she said she wasn't cold and worked until dark when Ethan started the car, insisting it was time to leave for Washington.

It was one of the least important jobs demanding attention at the time, but if the place started to look better from the outside in, it would speak well for the inn-to-be and it met an immediate psychic need, delineating the perimeter of the new future in shiny black, outlining it before filling in the colors.

Lucy, who was studying art in Florence at that time, offered to look around Italy and France for ideas and paint wall decorations when she came home. The tone of her voice said she knew all about the project from Amanda and Ethan, that they were appalled and thought we had made the mistake of our lives. Half the time I agreed with that, but couldn't see a way out now. "I thought you liked art museums and editing books," Lucy said before hanging up.

There were setbacks from every possible direction. If it wasn't the opening of duck hunting season, then it was goose, deer, dove, or rockfish season, or something else to do with local customs. Celebrating the Fourth of July around here, for example, starts a good week out. People knock off work early to stock in supplies, set up lawn furniture or the boat, repair fishing gear, and start cooking. If that's the week you think you need a new well dug or a building inspection, it's better to forget the idea and work on something else or, better yet, join the party.

And I still didn't see quite why, as people kept telling us, we needed a plumber, except to put in the pipes and drains for the bathrooms, maybe a new faucet in the kitchen.

The kitchen posed an interesting problem. Our living quarters occupied what was probably the original kitchen with its defunct chimney, once for a cookstove, more recently a winter home for snakes. A five-by-twelve-foot pantry between our space and the dining room had been converted in the 1930s, to judge by the sink, into the kitchen, so we were stuck.

Hugo sketched plans for a miniature professional kitchen, all stainless steel with a commercial range and sizable restaurant fridge, plus dishwasher and shelving. With a door to the dining room and another to the hall, in addition to a big window at the far end, space was ridiculously tight. He got everything to fit on his plans but looking them over I noticed that there wasn't enough clearance to open the oven or dishwasher doors. He rearranged everything until it all fit and we triple-checked the measurements. The much harder question was how to make it happen cheaply.

A kitchen, so important to a bed-and-breakfast, the nerve center really, from which Hugo planned to serve discriminating palates from breakfast through tea to candlelight dinners, and subject to health department inspection, had to be up to a certain standard. Fortunately the small commercial range and the fridge were less expensive than high-end household versions. Hugo found steel shelving at a home supply store at a fraction of the cost of professional kitchen design wares. That left countertops, another potential sinkhole for the budget. It occurred to Hugo that his brother Bobby, a racecar builder, could help out and Bobby willingly agreed to construct stainless steel countertops around the home supply store sink.

Rick later laid a handsome cobalt-blue tile backsplash above Bobby's countertop. Even with all the economies, Hugo was ever more worried about costs and suggested that we scale back the baths: The guests could share.

Absolutely not, I argued, insisting on private baths long before coming across a study of bed-and-breakfast guests that listed their top priority as a private bath. Personally, I never did like walking around in my bathrobe in front of strangers, the way you may have to do at an English inn or a bed-and-breakfast with a shared bath. In such situations, a friend once advised me, correct behavior is to wear a heavy robe and if you encounter anyone, no greeting is expected, just keep your eyes straight ahead.

Eyes straight ahead. The thought reminded me that Hugo seemed to be keeping his eyes straight ahead as we passed in the yard or the house, or ate a quick hamburger together, standing over the grill in the driveway at the end of the day. Eyes straight ahead, no talking. I worried that the stresses of the work and the expense were causing our relationship to take an ominous turn. Unless it meant the opposite, the evolution of the relationship to a higher state where much communication is nonverbal. Or it could just mean he was tired. The trouble was I didn't know which. I said something.

"It's just a phase," he answered, looking out the window. "It's just the way things are right now."

The Bull Crap Café

AT LEAST THE HOUSE WAS STANDING STRAIGHT. BUCK and Larry even knew a plumber. "There's only two good plumbers anywhere around here," Larry offered when he and Buck stopped by to see how the foundation was holding up. "Take your pick. Find them eating breakfast around six a.m., down at the Bull Crap."

"Pardon?"

"Bull Crap Café, town of Trappe, fifteen miles down the road . . . if you can get going that early." He gave me their names.

I decided to try calling them up. The first of the two, George, agreed to meet at noon on a Friday at our place. He had worked nearby and everyone I asked said good things about him.

His truck pulled into the driveway at 11:56, an encouraging sign. We shook hands and walked through the house. Hugo and I took turns explaining the plans for a bed-and-breakfast, where we needed a new bath in the upstairs sitting room and about cutting the large bathroom in half to make a third bath. He was silent.

Coming back downstairs, my nervous small talk bounced off him like pebbles off a Humvee and echoed around the empty rooms. We came to a stop in the parlor. He cast a cool, appraising eye over us.

"We'll do it. But you'll lose ceilings or floors. Take your pick."

I explained that the original plaster and the pine flooring were important to the ambience, to what people expected when they came to a bed-and-breakfast, and told him the bricks were made right on the property from the clay soil and the oak beams came from local trees, and about the integrity of the original building, its place in history, the importance of preserving it. George waited patiently until I finished.

"Ceilings or floors. Otherwise we can't get in to run the pipes. Some might run the pipes right up the inside walls, but I won't do that. You wouldn't like it either."

"How much?"

"Ten thousand, maybe. Can't really tell until we get into it."

Like the foundation contractor, he worked on "time and materials," meaning no contract, no set price. If you don't like the local system, you can bring in your own workers from the Western Shore, put them up at a motel, as some people did. Even if you can afford a work crew's living expenses, other come-heres cautioned, outsiders can have a slow time getting their construction permits approved. Worse yet, you won't have anyone to call in an emergency.

Territoriality is the issue. If they haven't worked at your place, forget calling them in an emergency. They take care of their own.

I called up the other plumber for a comparative bid. The following week he arrived, spent five minutes looking around and said maybe he could start before the end of the year but would charge $20,000.

I called George back to tell him the job was his, but couldn't reach him. Two calls a week for four weeks. The office staff always promised to give him my message. Something was fishy.

With the foundation work finished and the new bathrooms framed up, time would soon be wasting. Slowly it dawned on me that the two plumbers talked over breakfast at the café and were not pleased I had contacted both of them, taking up their time.

I decided to try a ploy that sometimes worked at my day job. Call very early, before the office staff arrives, and you might find the head of the company there working alone, even answering the phone.

George probably got up around five-thirty, got to the Bull Crap by six, to the office by six-thirty. I set my alarm for six.

Sitting down at the kitchen table with coffee, paper, and pencil, I jotted notes. I knew what to say, it was how to say it. At six-thirty-five, I dialed.

On the first ring, he answered. There was no mistaking his voice.

"George?"

"Yes." It was a wary yes.

I started to identify myself but he remembered. The bed-and-breakfast.

"We would like you to do the work if you are still willing."

Silence.

"We would like you to do the work because of your out-standing reputation."

More silence.

"And of course we will follow your advice," I added in a rush. "Would you prefer ceilings or floors removed?"

"Ceilings."

I thanked him and offered to send a deposit. Not necessary, he said. I assured him we would take the ceilings down right away, no problem. Hugo, I didn't say, had never taken down a ceiling in his life, but maybe he could learn fast.

"One more thing."

"Yes?"

"You need a new well, more capacity. Might as well get a new hot water heater while you're at it. Don't want guests at that B&B of yours running out of hot water. Call me when the well's in and we'll start."

Hugo came into the kitchen as I was hanging up and headed for the coffeepot. I waited until he sat down at the table.

"So?"

"Great news. George will do the work. All you have to do is take down the front and back hall ceilings and the kitchen ceiling first, and we need a new well."

"Great," he said, matching my upbeat denial of the bad news.

It was a bad news time. A few days later Hugo and Rick measured out the old shed. The new well required a larger well tank, and with the larger hot water heater it would all be impossibly tight in the small space. Poking around, they also discovered that powder post beetles (who ever heard of them?) had finished off the lower third of the vertical supports for the structure. It was more or less resting on nothing.

When George dropped by, he pointed out that the oil furnace was likely to quit any day now, and the shed foundation was cracked and sinking as well. He wouldn't install the new equipment over it if it was his house, but, hey, our choice.

Hugo paid the penalty fees and dipped into his small retirement savings. The contractor returned to build the new shed. To save money Hugo would install the floor and interior walls while the new well was being drilled.

It was a perfect, early September day. The workers, usually on the job by seven, at latest by nine if they had to pick up supplies or check on someone else's job, were nowhere in sight. We assumed it was another no-show day. These were an exasperation but Hugo never phoned them unless there were two in a row, which meant they were sandwiching in another job and if you didn't call them on it two days would lead to three, four, a week or more.

After painting primer on some siding to save the work crew time, Hugo went inside to make more coffee and switched on the TV. He called me over as the second plane hit the World Trade Center.

Fifteen minutes later the phone rang. The contractor wanted to let us know the crew was on its way, they were running late because of problems at another site. This was a first, consideration spurred by the stunning calamity.

In an hour they arrived and Hugo went outside. The contractor's sons, his work crew, stood in a tight, silent group staring at the ground. The contractor and Hugo exchanged a few words. After a few more minutes the contractor signaled the end of the impromptu mourning. "I say we nuke 'em." As if on cue everyone strapped on toolbelts, climbed ladders, and got to work.

Four months later George and his helpers finished installing the brand-new bathrooms. The combination of old and new, original floors and windows, along with quietly new fixtures and white brass, came together better than I had hoped, a pleasant surprise. Also in their places, glinting importantly and expensively, were the new hot water heater, the new well tank, and the new furnace—all in the new shed.

George himself arrived to supervise the first firing of the furnace, now attached to the old pipes and old radiators, which no longer tipped so badly because the repair of the damaged floor joists more or less leveled the floors. The January day was unusually cold and he found Hugo in a parka, cap, and gloves, suspended high on a makeshift scaffolding, scraping the two-story ceiling in the secret backstairs.

George walked back and forth in the upstairs hall, taking in Hugo at every pass as he checked the antiquated system of pipes and radiators. While his helper and I rushed up and down the stairs to make sure everything held, he fired the furnace. Soon the all-important flow of hot water into pipes and radiators resounded softly through the house. The old pipes, and everything else, held. The house started to warm up.

We shook hands and he drove off. He didn't want payment; he'd send a bill. Hugo had paid $2,000 up front for supplies, but after that George did not want more payments.

Worrisome as hell, but we didn't know what to do about it.

Six weeks later his bill for the balance of the work came. It was February again, one year after the place had become ours. Taking a work break around four in the afternoon, we walked down to the village post office, by now a weekly ritual, to see if the bill was there.

"If it's here, don't tell me," I said, suddenly weary. For the first time outside the office, I felt a sharp pain starting along my right temple and running down into the back of my neck, a migraine. Hugo unlocked the mailbox.

"Let's get this over with." He fumbled with the mailbox key and pulled out a small yellow envelope, hand addressed. That was it: I saw George's name in small block letters in the upper corner.

Hugo ripped it open and his eyes fixed on the page. We'd been up and down ladders all day, patching plaster and, in between, removing and cleaning door hardware, a seemingly endless stream of time-consuming, trivial tasks, the kind of detail that would make or break the place as a bed-and-breakfast. In other words, the kind of soul-numbing work they fast-forward on home restoration TV shows. We were six months behind schedule and falling more behind every day. I asked him again, less than pleasantly, not to tell me.

"Look," Hugo said, holding up a tissue-thin sheet. Handwritten were our names, address, and this. Balance due, $9,480.

I looked again. It was a gift beyond belief. We hugged.

Hugo stuck the bill in his jacket pocket and I saw the weariness in his eyes evaporate. We strolled back to the house, enthusing over a feeble sunset and the bracing wind. This entirely unexpected act of kindness was the sort of thing you might read about, but never seems to actually happen.

George himself worked long hours, had bills of his own to pay, a daughter to send to college. I asked myself why he did it and guessed that it had to do with the day he came to fire the furnace and saw Hugo working alone in the twenty-degree house. He saw and understood. He knew we couldn't afford help and he knew from experience that after hours of working under those conditions you have to warm your feet and hands slowly in warm water, as Hugo did every night for weeks that winter in a friend's bathtub.

This bathtub belonged to Ellen, who had just showed up in our driveway one late fall day. Getting out of her car, she'd called, "Hugo?"

He came from the garage to see who it was. "Ellen?"

"What are *you* doing here?" she asked.

"What are *you* doing here?" he answered.

Ellen was an avid reader who had frequented Hugo's bookstore with her daughters. He explained what we were up to and she said she had a weekend house less than a mile up the road. Casting a quick eye over our house that day from the driveway, she had asked, "Do you need a place to stay?"

It wasn't two weeks before we moved into her guest cottage. Hugo got cleaned up that first night, shaved, did his laundry, and we sat down to dinner in a warm room where we didn't need jackets and boots. "The bookstore and bookstore friends are still with us," he said simply.

I couldn't think of any way to repay George's favor so as soon as we both had money in the bank, Hugo and I wrote out checks, half each, and drove down to the town of Trappe to leave them in his mailbox.

The road passed long stretches of fields with glimpses of icy bay. George's house, a small brick ranch, was surrounded by fields and bay. I thought his understanding of our situation and generosity must have originated here, where he grew up, where his father ran the business before him in unforgiving isolation, a place of limited possibilities.

The Bay

HUGO SANDED, FILLED, AND RESANDED THE WOODWORK in the dining room. Examining it in the bright morning light as guests would see it, I decided to go over it again, trying to erase more of the deep ugly marks, not the small gentle ones, the patina of people and time.

He didn't mind my going over his work, but when he went over my spackling of the doors, I lost it. I took off a clog and heaved it at the door, cracking the new paint and taking out a chunk of wood. Seeing that only irritated me more, and I felt worse still when he quietly started repairing it. I ranted and said that he was just a better person than I was. Not everyone can be so calm, even, controlled, and such a perfect spackler.

"You care more about this house than you do about me," I yelled before aiming the second clog at him. I banged out the screen door and headed down to the water.

He's acting like a moody husband with a mistress, I thought. Too bad I had to spend all week in the city earning money to help support this project. Could he be taking advantage of that? Again I considered the possibility that work and stress were driving us into separate, lonely worlds. What a perfect irony if we shore up this nice old house and in the process damage our relationship beyond repair.

Often these days, I found myself walking down to the water's edge, for a few minutes or an hour. It always helped to clarify my objectives, the consoling sight of this geological marvel that surrounds our finger of land on three sides. From the dock where I like to stand, you can see the water turn almost any shade of blue, silver, white, gray, orange, mauve, pink, or black. Depending on the weather and time of day, it changes quickly, slowly, always unpredictably. On the most ordinary of afternoons it will surprise with a showing of luminous pale green, reflecting early spring light off the maples, oaks, and willows leafing out along the shoreline.

The largest estuary in North America, two hundred miles long, four thousand miles square, the Chesapeake Bay spans an astonishing 11,600 miles of coastline. Formed by glacial melt at the end of the last Ice Age, about 10,000 years ago, the bay is the drowned valley of the mighty Susquehanna River. Long before rising seas flooded the river valley, a meteorite carved out the mouth about 35 million years ago, to the south where the estuary opens to the Atlantic Ocean.

Much of the bay is shallow, less than thirty feet deep, and in places you can wade far out before the depth increases much over five feet. The shallowness of these warm, partly salt and partly fresh waters nurtures a magnificent ecosystem of fish, fowl, and plant life. There are hundreds of species of finfish and shellfish, thirty kinds of waterfowl alone. There are diving ducks, such as the canvasbacks and redheads, with their legs far back under their bodies to help them dive deep for food, and dabbling ducks, with their legs more centrally located for walking, such as mallards and black ducks. There are gorgeously plumed wood ducks, mergansers, Canada and snow geese, mute and tundra swans. Among the most beautiful of water birds, the great blue heron and the snowy egret inhabit the region for part or all of the year in the company of little blue herons, laughing gulls, oystercatchers, swallows, pelicans, cormorants, sandpipers, plovers, bald eagles, and ospreys.

That splendid raptor, the osprey, also known as the seahawk or fish eagle, was once in decline. Intensive study revealed that the pesticide DDT caused the shells of osprey eggs to become fragile and easily broken, resulting in "egg failure." Since the banning of DDT, ospreys have resurged and are more abundant now on the Chesapeake Bay than anywhere else in the world. Osprey pairs, which mate for life, return to the bay every March from the Caribbean and South America to occupy the same nest and hatch their cinnamon-brown eggs. Even with an improved environment, they have a much harder life and obstacles than we humans typically do.

Contemplating all this, I think, should be enough to catapult anyone into a permanent state of gratitude, not to say renewed loyalty to one's mate.

Whenever I take time to consider it, the bay's huge beauty and riches fill me with awe and hope. With its distinctive, extravagant flora and fauna, the bay once defined an entire culture centered on shipping, agriculture, fishing, and later crabbing and oystering, that spanned centuries. By 1900 a second culture appeared, one of recreation, and these two cultures now coexist side by side and compete with each other for diminishing resources. There are bay work boats and bay pleasure boats, bay industries and agriculture, bay tourism and development.

Following construction in the 1950s of the Chesapeake Bay Bridge, conveniently linking the Eastern Shore to the mainland, massive development got underway. Even still, stretches of bay and shoreline appear as untouched and picturesque as a century or more ago, if you know where to look.

Along with the new, traditions also survive, especially in the architecture of towns dating to the seventeenth century and in bay foods and bay cooking. At almost every dockside restaurant and crab house, a distinctive seasoning imparts zing to the famous steamed blue crabs and also to potatoes, corn, bread, eggs, popcorn, crackers, and anything else people want to put it on. A blend of spices, it usually includes coarse salt, mustard seed, paprika, black and red peppers, bay laurel, ginger, allspice, mace, and clove.

These days, of course, the defining force that was the bay is doing far less defining. It has been eaten up, like our house, from inside and out. Though saving a house, I remind myself, is nothing compared to saving a bay.

You would never guess from the developers' advertisements about the good life here or from the restaurants offering all the crabs you can eat that the bay is deathly ill. The trouble started long before a campaign to "Save the Bay" was launched in the 1970s. Every step of development from the steamships and railways in the nineteenth century to the cars, highways, and housing of the twentieth has contributed. By the 1970s the situation was critical and billions of dollars later the crisis is worse. No matter what the agencies working on the problems or responsible for them may say in their "cautiously optimistic" reports, the situation remains desperate.

The oysters are all but gone and the legendary blue crab, *Callinectes sapidus*, too. The name, given by a Smithsonian Institution scientist, comes from the Latin *sapidus*, meaning savory or tasty, and the Greek for beautiful swimmer. More than beautiful swimmers, they're beautiful, tasty swimmers and, like the taste of the oyster, the taste of crab only creates a desire for more—which helps matters not at all.

At the same time that the shellfish are disappearing, along with the submerged aquatic vegetation, or SAV, that is so important to the ecosystem, other forms of life have rebounded, notably the shad and striped bass. But even this is not a win-win . . .

A summer or so back, a neighbor close by on Edge Creek sighted a bullnose shark cruising off the end of his dock. What was a large shark doing up this shallow creek? "Very aggressive, the bullnose," the Department of Natural Resources advised when the sighting was reported. "Probably hungry, probably chasing striped bass."

And what are striped bass doing up this shallow creek? "They're hungry, too. Probably came up the creek to eat baby crabs," said the Department of Natural Resources.

In the 1980s, striped bass were in short supply from over-harvesting so fishing for striped bass, called rockfish locally, was banned. The fish rebounded in large numbers. A success story for the bass, but not for young blue crabs that hide in underwater grasses in the shallow, warm creeks.

Between the bass feasting on little crabs and the human passion for big crabs, a passion that depletes 75 percent of the bay's adult crab stock every year, one of the great glories of the bay is in dangerously short supply. To help meet summertime demand, crab is now shipped in from the Gulf of Mexico and South Asia.

Trying to help, the state offered to buy back crabbing licenses in 2009 from Maryland watermen. After consulting economists, who proposed a technique from game theory, the state asked each waterman to privately name his price. One crabber asked $425 million; others refused to bid altogether, saying the license was their link to the past, family and traditions. Said one, "I would feel like part of me was gone. . . This is what I am."

The native oysters are in even worse shape than the crabs. Overharvested since the late nineteenth century, and diseased more recently as a result of poor water quality, 98 percent of the oysters are gone. Go out on the water with Captain Wade Murphy on his skipjack, the traditional shallow-draft sailing boat used to harvest bay oysters, and he'll dredge for oysters, pulling up perhaps a dozen. Ten of the twelve will be dead. Other days he pulls up only empty shells.

Projects are underway to save the shellfish, such as building reefs for oyster beds and seeding with disease-resistant and nonnative species of oysters. This is a controversial issue, as no one can predict for certain what will happen once nonnative species are introduced. In another effort, the U.S. Army Corps of Engineers deposited a million oysters in the bay in the summer of 2004, hoping to increase the population. Within weeks, to the engineers' embarrassment, a raiding party of cownose rays, relatives of the stingray, came along and gobbled up about 750,000 of the young oysters, a feast that cost $45,000.

Beyond their exquisite flavor, the oysters are important for a much larger reason. They filter water for nutrients, such as algae, and in so doing help to clean the bay. Because an oyster can filter as much as five liters of water an hour, scientists believe that the once-vast oyster population filtered the entire volume of the bay's waters every three to four days. Oysters were so plentiful at one time that they formed shoals large enough to endanger ships. Overharvesting began after the Civil War with the advent of train service that rushed the oysters to market. Production peaked in the 1880s, when 20 million bushels of oysters a year were taken. Ever since, the harvest has declined.

So why not set up the grill on the lawn and eat more chicken until the shellfish rebound? Because chickens and lawns are part of the problem. The area's chicken farms—along with agriculture and lawns all up and down the watershed, including dairy farms in Pennsylvania—represent the single biggest cause of environmental damage to the bay because they produce runoffs of nitrogen from fertilizers and phosphorous from manure. The runoff into the bay and its creeks leads to algae overgrowth, or "blooms," which block light needed by other plant life. When the algae die and decompose, consuming oxygen in the process, further species are threatened.

A chicken tax is proposed by environmentalists to help clean up and truck away the manure. But housing development all along the shoreline, bringing more lawns and more fertilizer use, contributes excessive nutrients to the runoff as well. More paved roads, more auto emissions, more shopping centers, more sewage, and more stormwater from all around the 64,000-square-mile watershed of the Chesapeake contribute chemical contaminants, too.

The largest river that drains into the bay, the Susquehanna once brought a rush of clean water. In time, the river was dammed, the flow of cleansing water diminished, and the river itself began contributing pollution; by 2005 the Susquehanna was listed as the country's most endangered river. By 2006 the Chesapeake Bay Foundation ranked the bay's health at 29 on a scale of 100. Although this represents a 2-point improvement over previous years, underwater grasses scored 18, shad got a 10, and the native oyster scored 4. The cleanup is far behind schedule. By 2010 the bay was supposed to be clean enough to be taken off the federal list of "dirty waters." No one expects that goal to be met. The federal Environmental Protection Agency is considering moving the deadline to 2020, by which time many say the bay and its tributaries may be beyond saving and leading the nonprofit Chesapeake Bay Foundation to file suit against the agency for failing to enforce the Clean Water Act.

And that's what happened to the Chesapeake Bay, or the *Chesepiooc* as the Algonquians called it, which some say means Great Shellfish Bay.

Much of the world chooses to live where land and water meet. In the United States the majority of the population lives within fifty miles of an ocean, bay, or the shores of the Great Lakes. As naturalist Tom Horton points out, people are drawn to this edge "because it's beautiful and just plain more interesting than anywhere else."

With human habitation taking a heavy toll and continued population growth of about 170,000 people a year along the Chesapeake watershed, it isn't hard to see the bay's very beauty and interest as its ultimate tragic flaw.

Captain Murphy and his family have fished the bay waters for three generations. Over the years he has developed perspective on adversity. When his skipjack sank in a squall, he got it pulled up, declared a National Historic Landmark, and with the help of preservation funds he restored it. Now he puts it to new use with excursions and environmental lectures to tourists.

"It isn't complicated," he sums up as we come ashore following an afternoon with him on the *Rebecca T. Ruark*. "If everyone would just stop making three stupid mistakes—stop damming the rivers, stop overfishing, and stop putting things in the bay that don't belong there—the bay *might* recover and the shellfish might come back."

Family, Family

WHEN RICK ARRIVED AGAIN ON ONE OF HIS MANY
visits, he looked around and sighed. "The area is so WT."
Huh? Hugo said.
"You know, WT. White trash."

"If you like it, fine," my sister said when we thought the
place was really starting to spruce up in the second year of
work. "But I could *never* live here."
A third relative was even less subtle. We were eating in
a café in St. Michaels when he announced, "This town looks
like shit."
Back at the house, Hugo needed a few glasses of wine
while we discussed this comment. Not long after, the *New
York Times* described St. Michaels as "picture perfect . . . a
place of waterfront sunsets and white sails," and the area
was listed in a sleek travel magazine as one of the ten most
romantic places in the country for a weekend getaway, not
to mention the entire town's inclusion on the National Register of Historic Places. I thought of the trees, fields, woods,

creeks, coves, marshes, and painterly stretches of open bay. Something didn't add up.

Along with small, simple houses and a few trailer homes, there are the old estates, private airstrips, the weekend houses of well-known public figures in business, sports, and politics that eventually included then–Vice President Dick Cheney and Secretary of Defense Donald Rumsfeld. The Cheney and Rumsfeld houses sit practically next door to each other, less than a thirty-minute helicopter ride from Washington. "Outside the blast zone" was a popular surmise.

Was it because we, the family financial failures, wound up here that the rest of the family took more than a dim view of the project and even the whole setting? The town was guilty by association with us. We finished a bottle of wine and mulled the question into the night.

Subliminally I was inclined to like the place, having first seen the bay by boat and later by car, although I hardly knew where I was that day when I drove across the Bay Bridge to St. Michaels to meet James Michener as he was starting work on his epic novel *Chesapeake*. At the time I was an assistant book editor for the *Washington Post* and liked to get away from the desk now and again when I could come up with a good enough reason. Michener's arrival on the Eastern Shore was news, though no one seemed to know exactly what he was up to. Arriving in St. Michaels early, I walked around and asked. "One doesn't ask," a shopkeeper said.

Michener was sixty-nine. We met at the house he was renting on the Miles River, talked, ate crab cakes and French fries at the Town Dock, and returned to his house to talk some more. He spoke freely about writing, research, how he approached projects, about success and fear of failing. He could have retired after his first book appeared, *Tales of the South Pacific*, which won a Pulitzer Prize, sold millions of copies, and became a popular film and Broadway musical, but he kept on researching and writing his massive volumes of fiction and nonfiction. It came back, he said, to a childhood spent in and out of foster homes with some bad luck companions.

"An essential fact about me," he offered, "is that I've always known people can end on the ash heap." Mostly he talked about the bay, which he first encountered fifty years before. Spurred by news of its despoliation, he returned.

The day before we met, he had explored with a guide stretches of the Choptank River that looked exactly as they would have 150 years before. He expressed Huck Finn–ish delight at that thought, saying he was enjoying himself "100 percent more than expected."

On his desk I saw a copy of John Barth's *Sotweed Factor* and an array of old maps. Michener told me that on the earliest maps the bay's western shore was inscribed in lowercase letters while the Eastern Shore was always capitalized. His expression clearly said, *And with good reason*.

This is a place that grows on you, gets into your psyche, I realized. Here was a man who could go anywhere in the world, and did. The Eastern Shore and the bay get to you, if you let them. It's the reason they ship Old Bay Seasoning around the world to the nostalgic who have experienced the bay and left it.

• • •

A black car with tinted windows eased over the crushed oyster shells, dirt, and weeds that passed for our driveway and came to a stop. Slowly, an older man in massive black wraparound sunglasses, baseball cap, polo shirt, and gray flannel dress slacks got out.

When he took off the sunglasses I recognized my father-in-law, a short, frail man with pale blue eyes and a kind face. I set down my paintbrush and pulled off the green surgical mask he had given me.

"Oh, it's you," he said. "What the hell happened to him?" He was looking at Hugo, whose hair, skin, and clothing were all powdery white.

We didn't keep the drywall finisher long, I explained, only long enough for Hugo to learn how to do it. I didn't say that we were way over budget and that the drywall finisher made me uneasy. Everyone said he was the best in the business, just a harmless eccentric who worked by night, stripped naked. By day he slept in his car, which was decked out with pillows, clothes, food, water, stacks of yellowed newspapers, and a small TV. Sometimes you'd see him filling up at the gas station or catch sight of his car parked down some shady, out-of-the-way lane.

Hugo pointed out to his dad that the car engine was still running and the driver, a colleague, had not gotten out. "Doesn't Dr. M. want to come inside with you and see the place?"

"No. I won't be long."

I remembered my sister's first visit. Is this a family trait or what?

Hugo Senior walked the perimeter of the house, taking in the new construction and the remains of the old shed stacked by the garage. He climbed the front porch steps, took off his sunglasses and peered inside.

Coughing and wiping plaster dust from his face with a bandanna, Hugo Junior walked beside him. I trailed close enough to listen but far enough back to stay out of any "discussion." When his dad turned abruptly and headed back down the porch steps for the waiting car, Hugo stopped coughing enough to say, "Come on, Dad, I'll show you around inside."

"No, thanks. Got to get back to Washington."

"But you just got here. Don't you want something to drink or eat?"

"No, thanks." He reached for the car door.

"Did I ever tell you . . ." His father stood there, seemingly lost in thought.

"Dad? Maybe you should come inside and rest before you leave."

"No, we're leaving in a minute. As I was saying, did I tell you about the time I got a call from the State Department? They wanted me to go to the Mideast, maybe to operate on someone. When we landed, I found out we were in Baghdad and that the president of the country had disappeared. This other guy was in charge, Saddam Hussein. Some thuggish bodyguards drove me across the city to an impressive building and took me to an upper floor. I came into a room and the first thing I saw was a circle of eighteen gilt chairs. I recognized physicians from all the major countries sitting there. Then I noticed at the head of the room, up on a platform in a big bed, was Hussein. He was having back problems. They wanted a diagnosis from each doctor.

"It was clear to me, after examining him, that if he rested he'd be fine. I didn't want to operate. I said so. The others agreed.

"Then the toughs who were guarding us drove us to a hotel, to get some sleep, before they took us out to an island. They pretty much had control of us. We had to go. When we got there, I saw a tent and there was liquor, anything you could possibly want to drink. I didn't know what they were going to do. They built a big fire. I was kind of relieved when they used the fire to cook fish. We had a feast. After we ate, they gave us gifts and drove us back to the airport. I was happy to be going home . . ."

He looked around then, coming back to the present. "Don't know what made me think about that—" He got in the car.

As the door closed, Hugo quickly asked, "Well, what do you think?"

"Probably a good investment, if you ever get it fixed up and ever get anyone to come out here."

The car rolled down the driveway.

In the hunch of his shoulders, it was clear how Hugo felt. Years of dreams, plans, and work merited a ten-minute visit.

"Honey, you know that's as expansive as he gets," I said, aware that both of us could not afford to be down at the same time or the project was doomed. I was always encouraging him to work faster, because every day we weren't open for business cost double: money out, no money in. Hugo could always go back to the job he disliked and I could try to stick it out at the office if it came to that, but turning back now would be admitting failure and opening the door wide to bigger failures. "The only people who never fail are those who never try," Mark Twain said, a quotation that I taped to the kitchen door in the first days of the project.

Hugo walked on ahead of me. He knew we needed to finish this and I did, too. I thought about the glorious bookstore days, then about Hugo in cooking school working alongside "the kids," the other students half his age, then sweating it out in restaurant kitchens and enduring the humiliations of the catering business. He needed a success soon.

I was enthusiastic about the bed-and-breakfast for my own reasons, but being his idea, it weighed more on him. In this we were typical of couples who start a bed-and-breakfast. One person instigates it, the other goes along.

"Hey," I called to his back. "Your dad didn't say it's a stupid mistake." This characteristic remark was probably easier to take if you hadn't heard it all your life. My father-in-law mostly meant it as a joke. If you're going to make a mistake, please don't make it a stupid one. But Hugo had trouble seeing it that way.

I hesitated, trying to get at the truth. In his late eighties, his dad no longer saw well enough to drive himself around the Beltway, across the Bay Bridge, and down Route 50 to our back roads. He asked a friend to make the three-hour round-trip with him, without even stopping for a rest. He didn't call the project stupid. He even said something positive about it. Hugo was too close to see.

"It seems like he damned us with faint praise, but . . ." I thought for a moment, aware that this was a very important moment. Hugo was on the edge. I needed exactly the right idea and the right word to say it. Then I had it. It was a sort of benediction.

He wasn't listening. "A what?"

I repeated slowly. *Ben-e-dict-ion*. His blessing, a cool one. It was as much as he could give, something like a light kiss on the forehead by someone whose focus is elsewhere. There was no hint that day of what he really thought, what he might do.

Take what you get, I could hear my mother saying. *And like what you take*.

Pennies and Nails

UP ON THE ROOF, IN THE FIREPLACE, UNDER THE PORCH, pennies by the hundred were everywhere. Good luck, I hoped, and left them there. There were nails everywhere too, in the floors, doors, walls, and ceilings. Hugo pulled out hundreds of old, hand-forged nails and piled them up in buckets.

Why anyone needed that many nails was a mystery. And why did every wall in the house look like someone had kicked

it or thrown something at it? I had time to consider the question as I worked on repairs. Most of the time we divided up
the chores, except for the very, very dreadful ones that neither
of us could bear to do alone, like collecting discarded syringes,
contraceptives, and plastic bags from around the yard. We
filled seven trash cans with empty beer and soda cans.

Once all this was cleared, smaller objects began to emerge,
shards of blue and white dishware, spoons, children's marbles,
old bottles, and a tiny porcelain friar, a bright expression glim-
mering on his round, grimy face. The house mascot. I washed
off the dirt and set him on a shelf surrounded by pennies.

There were oyster shells, too, a commonplace along the
bay, where shell mounds mark early Indian settlements and
later centers of commercial oystering, times when oysters
were so abundant that a good eater might devour as many as
a hundred at a sitting. The quantity of shells I saw suggested
that previous residents, including the minister who first lived
in our house with his mother and sister, and those who followed him enjoyed oysters as much as anyone.

Our attempts at rescuing the house from nature were
apparently unending. A tug-of-war was in full swing long
after we thought we were in charge, with snakes, vines, wasps,
and wood rot all trying to claim shares. Six brown turkey buzzards, beaked ellipses—I'm sorry to use the word—*lurked* in
a half-dead cherry tree near the front door.

I regretted a lack of sympathy for these fellow travelers but
couldn't help it. The sight of them perched high in the branches
day after day sent shivers of foreboding through me. Fortunately, a storm blew the cherry tree down and the buzzards

departed, at first for a tree next door, then, as activity peaked around our place, they moved farther away and stayed there.

Reclaiming the house from former inhabitants seemed easier than taking it back from nature, but in the end it took longer and called for different tactics.

One Saturday afternoon an attractive thirtyish man came by and sat down on the porch floor, yoga-style in the half-lotus. He heard we were looking for a painter. He spoke well and was cleanly dressed in khakis and a white shirt that hung too loosely on him, as if he weren't eating enough. He said he used to live in our house and would really like to be around again. He was having trouble getting his head together, but when he did, he wanted to do some of the painting. Hugo finally got rid of him by suggesting he write up a proposal for his work.

Another Saturday, which seemed to be the day for visiting, a man wearing a sleeveless undershirt, short shorts that could have been underwear, and flip-flops showed up. He sported tattoos head-to-foot of pirates and coiled snakes with long forked tongues.

Hugo noticed him first and went forward. This man also said he used to live in the house and if we wouldn't mind, he'd like to take a look around.

"Maybe some other time," Hugo said, holding his ground on the path between the man and the kitchen door. Hugo is six feet tall and had developed some muscle from the construction work. This man had a full half-foot on him and about forty pounds.

As our visitor launched into reminiscences of good times at the house, he kept edging closer until he and Hugo faced each other inches apart. He said he would appreciate seeing the room that used to be his, the one at the top of the backstairs.

"It's all torn up right now. We're working on it," Hugo lied.

"Hey, okay." He held out his hands, palm up, and turned to go, then stopped.

"Okay if I come back later, maybe bring along a metal detector, take a look around?"

Sure, Hugo said.

These visitors made me long for other visitors, pleasant company who might offer a word of encouragement now and then. There weren't any ghosts around, as most of our neighbors claimed to have. So I invented a ghost of a former resident, Mrs. Jefferson, whose mother had acquired the property from the Methodist Church in the 1930s and whose son sold the place to us. Neighbors said that in her day it had been a fine house. It was easy to imagine what she would think. Her voice would have my grandmother's soft, Southern cadence. *If I may say so*, she would have remarked once the tattooed man left, *I did not approve of some of the goings-on around here. I most certainly did not* . . .

As I went about estimating how much fabric it would take to improvise a swag across the four bay windows, seven feet high, in the sitting room and the two front-facing windows, I knew what she would advise. *Measure twice, cut once, dearie.*

When Hugo and the rest of the family heard about Mrs. Jefferson, they didn't seem alarmed or, if they were, they didn't let on. I overheard Hugo telling family that he saw it more as a reflection of the character of the house and how hard the work was, rather than someone losing her marbles.

Lucy called right up though, asking about it. "Really interesting," she said. "Be sure to let me know if the House Spirit says anything else."

It was time to choose paint colors and I quickly learned what any decorator could have told me in a minute, a swatch is one thing, color on a wall can be something else entirely. For the woodwork throughout the house, I tried out Simply White (too white), Old Ivory (too yellow), Vanilla Ice Cream (far too yellow), Bone White (chalky), and Navajo White (pinkish) before finding Linen White. Then I had to learn that a semigloss finish was much better than high gloss, which only highlighted the wood's imperfections. The choice of a white proved the most challenging, but it went much the same way in each room.

In the dining room, I saw no need to try to improve on a great master and intended to simply copy what Claude Monet had chosen for his own home at Giverny, a blue-and-yellow color scheme. The five yellows I tried were much too bright. Eventually, I realized that one of the discarded whites, Old Ivory, matched almost exactly the yellow walls pictured in one of my favorite books, *Monet's Table*. Some people (smarter than I), a bed-and-breakfast guest later informed me, take the book right into the paint store, have the color scanned and the color custom-mixed.

Elsewhere in the house, where I'd painted test patches on the walls, I asked anyone who stopped by which they liked best. Usually everyone agreed on what was the most appropriate and serene color.

But what everyone from neighbors to friends, family, guests, and would-be innkeepers really wanted to discuss was this: How will you make it? What does an enterprise like this cost and can you make any money at it?

So here it is. Naturally, getting started cost much more than estimated and took much longer. We had never heard of the 3-2 Rule, which decrees that any home project will take three times longer and cost double your estimate. We created a new rule, the 4-6 Rule. I have yet to meet an innkeeper who opened on time and on budget, even with spreadsheets, but if you are more precise with your estimates than we were and factor in enough margin for overruns, you can avoid surprises like these:

The house, purchased in 2001 in "as-is" condition	$110,000
Estimated cost of renovations	$25,000–$30,000
Actual cost of renovations	$90,000 and two years of Hugo's time
Estimated time to complete the work and open for business	6 months
Actual time from purchase to opening	2 years

Certainly it's possible to buy an up-and-running bed-and-breakfast, if you can afford that. Either way, be sure to consider *why* people would want to come and stay at your place. It should be near a resort or tourist area, on a popular travel route, or in proximity to other attractions, such as a historic town, a college, or areas of natural beauty.

What, then, can you expect if you find a place, obtain a license (in our town the house has to be historic or deemed "interesting" by a county agency to qualify), open for business, advertise, and eventually guests start to come? To make money, the general rule is that you need at least five rooms with a decent occupancy rate. A key factor is how many nights a year you can reasonably expect to be booked, based on other inns and businesses in the area, and on what you are offering. Fewer than five rooms can be borderline and is often considered a hobby, though an income-producing one. Fewer than three rooms is considered companionship. Technically, we were at the hobby borderline, but hoping to cover expenses and get lucky, with plans of one day making a go of it. More recently, with the higher cost of real estate, this has become trickier to do.

Another factor to consider is furnishing the place. A bed-and-breakfast requires that charm quotient, an elegant aura of the romantic, the bygone, the exotic, or the rustic, a pleasing suggestion of "elsewhere," that allows guests to escape from the everyday. And that, everyone who knew of our scheme warned, is really going to be expensive.

No, it won't, I answered, because I knew our budget and the secondhand shop in our village where unbelievable finds awaited anyone willing to do a little work on the furniture you bought there. I also knew the family attics. Between my father-in-law and my own mother, I calculated that there was a staggering 178 years of living to draw on without even counting what had been passed on to them by their parents. So I started with what we already had and planned a short shopping list of lamps, linens, and new mattresses. Bed-and-breakfast guests rank good beds second only to private baths on their list of preferences, according to industry studies.

Another preference among guests, as it turns out, is for an absence of teddy bears, chintz, and bric-a-brac. Some guests will specifically inquire about this before booking as a prelude to asking about dust and allergens. For others it's a question of aesthetics. This was lucky for us, because my own strong preference was for a suggestion, an evocation of the past, not a full-blown set piece.

Even so, we were going to need a certain amount of stuff beyond my short list of basics. After exhausting the attics, I took frequent walks down to Julie's Oak Creek Sales to hunt for fixable chairs, tables, dressers, mirrors. In time we had to look further, stopping at thrift and used-furniture stores wherever we happened to be, usually on trips to and from the hardware and lumber supply stores.

The idea of saving a house that would otherwise bulk up a landfill is hugely appealing. Old houses also hold history and secrets that you can sense at every turn, in their nooks, their hand-hewn beams, windows, mantles, and unpredictable corners. I used to avoid impassioned conversations among home renovators, but I came to understand. It becomes an obsession with addictive rewards if things go well, a kind of gambling. No wonder saving old houses is an industry and a culture all its own, with blogs, Web sites, magazines, newsletters, TV shows, clubs, and stores.

The same rewards lie in preserving smaller objects, and an unexpected advantage of starting a bed-and-breakfast is that what could be a time-consuming, not to say expensive, hobby becomes your business. After more than a few futile efforts and mistakes, I began to get the hang of this new sport, sizing up quickly if a thrift store had something we needed and could work with. It might mean nothing more than reinforcing a shaky structure, a wobbly chair or table legs with L-brackets.

I explained to Hugo how I had seen my father do it. The first time Hugo tried, he screwed the brackets to the outside of the chair. "Think anyone will notice?" he said, reaching for the screwdriver to move them.

It might mean sanding a stained or chipped surface or just brushing on furniture stain to bring an old end table or bookcase back to life. At the home supply store I came across marker pens in many different wood finishes—oak, beech, mahogany, walnut, ash, cedar, redwood, cherry, and "colonial"—and bought them all. I walked around the house with these pens in my pockets, ready to touch up scratches on the thrift store furniture until it crossed a line in my estimation between neglected and well cared for.

Sometimes we returned from shopping empty-handed and frustrated, certain that although we had come far, the shoestring was just too short. A pleasing ambience was beyond our reach. How do you improvise a good, solid bed frame that also shows style? Then a real find would give us energy for more hunting. At a secondhand clothing store that also dealt in used rugs, books, and odd pieces of furniture, Hugo spotted some dining chairs shoved in a back corner.

Unpriced, they were wobbly and needed new upholstery, but their beautiful, spare grace would distract the eye from our undistinguished dining table. Hugo asked if they were for sale.

"They're in bad shape," the owner said. "Fifteen each?" Hugo paid for all six and picked up four, two in each arm, leaving me to follow him out of the store with two more. He hurried to load them into the truck, explaining that we needed to get out of there before the owner changed his mind. If they aren't Duncan Fife, he said, they're fine copies. I didn't know this famous furniture maker and asked how he knew. The usual, he said—a book.

One chair was covered in pale-green, moiré taffeta. I imagined the refined house from which it came, where no one ever spilled anything. For our purposes, I selected dark-blue velvet and Hugo showed me how to use the staple gun. The main rule was never hold it toward your face.

I cut out a rough square of velvet, stretched it tight, shut my eyes, and fired. The gun went off with a sharp bang. Opening my eyes, I saw that I half-missed the fabric. The second try was better and I stapled all around the bottom of the frame before turning the seat right side up to see the fabric bunched up. When I yanked it free from the staples, it ripped. My next chair was better and the fifth one looked almost professional. The green taffeta was simply too beautiful to cover over, so I left it.

The decorating, as it evolved, became a real witches' brew, with an antique Persian rug from Hugo's dad next to the thrift store dining table, lace handmade by Hugo's grandmother and mine alongside synthetic silk swags from the remnant table at the fabric store. I was especially proud of this imitation silk *couleur changeant*, which can be seen in portrait paintings by the Old Masters, who delighted in capturing the varied hues of this intricately woven fabric.

My remnant reflected rose and blue, picking up the colors planned for the sitting room. For the dining room's two huge windows, I found ready-made blue silk curtains that fit, so I splurged. When someone interested in such things asks if the curtains are silk, I'll ask them to guess which ones are the real thing.

The dining room became my favorite example of the witches' brew. A 1911 portrait of my father in his white christening dress, still in its original oval gilt frame, presides over a handsome, polished pewter candlestick from Julie's store that she sold to me for $7 because its mate was missing. On the mantle also are an antique English tea box, an anniversary gift from Hugo; blue-and-white pottery shards from the backyard; a sampling of hand-forged nails from the house; the iridescent feather of a wood duck that I found on a walk; and a bird's nest from the attic rafters, complete with the blue half-shell of a robin's egg.

On the other side of the room a somewhat hulking, late nineteenth–century buffet that once served as theater staging dominates. Hugo discovered this marble-topped wonder covered with dust in a barn in western Maryland and used it as the cash register counter in the bookstore for years before its fall from grace to kitchen work counter for the catering business. This was very hard on the buffet and before installing it in the bed-and-breakfast, I spent many days gluing broken pieces into place and applying furniture stain to bring it back. Oak for the doors, a darker walnut stain for some of the inlaid trim. On a band of badly nicked faux ebony, I tried a regular marker pen but it left a shiny scribble so I bought a small can of flat black paint and a fine brush to go over all this trim, which ran from one end of the buffet to the other. More inset wood with a marled surface required three different pens for the touch-up. When visitors compliment the piece, I can only smile. It took me almost as long to fix it up as for Hugo and Rick to rebuild the front porch.

Before opening, I scrutinized the dining room because guests would be sitting there in bright daylight for an hour or longer. They'd have time to look around and be pleased, or not. Most of the house's original light fixtures were missing by the time we came along, including the dining room chandelier. Where bare wires extended from a gap in the plaster ceiling we hung a reproduction wrought-iron chandelier with amber globes. This large room, which runs the width of the house, demanded a substantial light fixture and an antique, we learned in months of futile scouting, was much too expensive.

The reproduction looked all right at night, but I thought its newness showed by day. The dried flowers I strung into it began crumbling right away and I worried about pieces falling into the guests' breakfasts. Eventually, I hit on another idea. Gathering up my mother's red-handled rolling pin, an egg beater, wooden spoons, ravioli cutters from Hugo's aunt, a berry basket, and an old tin camp mug, I hung them in and around the chandelier and stood back. In an embassy dining room I had once seen something like this made with new cooking gadgets and I decided that whether or not my rustic version worked for anyone else, here it would stay.

Another source for décor turned out to be an architectural salvage business that opened up less than two hours away in the center of Baltimore. As green a business as could be, it sits in the shadow of the Ravens stadium. We made the round-trip at least five times to hunt for everything from doors to hinges, latch plates, and antique doorknobs. Wading with a flashlight through snow melt into one of their darkest, deepest warehouses, we came across a hoard of genuine, old interior shutters. Sadly, our house had once been outfitted with shutters inside as well as out, and either for modernizing or an economy of repair, every last one had been removed. The hinges still in place showed where a dozen interior sets, individually made for each window, had hung.

In the warehouse two pairs of solid mahogany shutters from someone else's house waited for us. They needed only scraping and painting to put in ours. I say "only" because the first set took about five hours' work but with experience Hugo did the second set in less than half the time. We also found several more sets of shutters that day for the exterior of the house. Of course you never know what surprising gifts you'll receive when you buy old things, and the shutters came complete with a baby bat clinging tightly to a slat. Hugo gently nudged it loose before laying the shutters in the bed of the truck.

This salvage business, called Second Chance, frequents buildings about to be demolished, strips away good windows, doors, bath and light fixtures, staircases, mantles, transoms, decorative architectural elements, metalwork, and lumber to resell. An entire surreal courtyard is filled with claw-footed bathtubs. Operating in several cities now, they hire and train unemployed local inner city residents to do the work.

Our pine front door, two inches thick, was salvaged from a 1901 Baltimore hotel scheduled for teardown. The business is booming and on our last visit they had expanded to five warehouses.

Good luck like that went into the mix, along with gifts from Hugo's beloved aunt. Zia Lillia had followed our progress at every phase, and although she was too ill to come visit from New Jersey, she kept asking how soon we would be in business and what we needed.

Her extra china, book cabinets, and lamps were the very vintage of the house. They filled in around the attic and thrift store finds, giving the house a truly settled feeling. Although she never said so directly, Zia Lillia, the Italian equivalent of a steel magnolia, wasn't happy that she didn't get to arrange her possessions in the new setting. *Could be worse*, I heard her say after I placed a cabinet in a corner of the small sitting room at the front of the house I called the parlor because that's what my grandmother called a like room in her house. The parlor was for company.

Setting a photograph of Zia Lillia in her schoolgirl dress, white stockings, and high-buttoned shoes inside the cabinet, I shuddered. As soon as I moved her to the fireplace mantle, I heard her say, *That's more like it. From here I can see and be seen . . .*

I moved on, filling overlooked nail holes as I planned the rest of the decoration and to take my mind off the boring work, pictured Zia Lillia meeting Mrs. Jefferson. In these encounters, as in life, Zia Lillia always got the last word.

If Mrs. Jefferson observed pleasantly over tea, *My house has come back, and I must say I'm rather pleased* . . . Zia Lillia would snap, *Your house? Yes, it's come back, no thanks to you.*

Sounds from the driveway brought me back to the present. I looked out and saw two trucks parked. Three men, smoking cigarettes, formed a half-circle around Hugo.

9

Pink Paint

"HAPPY NOW?" HUGO ASKED AS I JOINED HIM OUTSIDE. Two painter's assistants dragged on their cigarettes, flipped the burning butts into the garden, and followed their boss up onto the porch. We followed the painters. "I know I'm a little slow," Hugo was saying, "and like you said, if we have some help we can open a lot sooner."

Summer again—our second year of work on the house. With painting and finishing the walls and woodwork going slowly, it could mean another year before we opened. On the dining room alone Hugo spent four weeks. I assured him I was very happy and went back to see if the painters' cigarettes were still burning.

Greg, the painter, was in demand, with more jobs than he could get to, but he obviously felt sorry for us and our sad-sack house. He himself lived in a development of new houses many times the size of ours, we knew from the friends who recommended him. Greg didn't mind painting just the front façade of our house for now and would do the rest of the exterior when we could afford it. Only after they finished that and moved indoors did trouble start.

I found Greg offering sympathy to Hugo because he had the same problem with his wife—all the wacky paint colors she demanded. They were in the parlor and an assistant painter stared down at the bucket of paint, an old-fashioned hue called ashes of roses I had chosen for the walls, and then at Hugo. He didn't know about other guys, but personally he wouldn't be caught dead in a house with pink paint.

"Just paint it, Bunk," Greg ordered. "It's all green to me."

After the parlor they headed into the front hall with its twenty-foot ceiling in the stairway, and after that would come the upstairs hall. The painters moved with amazing speed. They finished the exterior in two days, the parlor in one, and they were starting on the hall as Hugo and I went out to buy more paint.

Weeks before, Lucy had arrived home from Italy and come straight to Royal Oak on a sweltering weekend to paint a fire screen and decorate the guest bedroom doors. Each guest room was named for a tree in the yard—Elm, Linden, Acorn—and for each of the grown children, in hopes that they would bond with the future family home. Lucy and I spent time in the cool of the air-conditioned public library studying tree books and she sketched leaves and acorns until she came up with images that she thought were both true-to-life and artistic. She stenciled them on the doors and painted them with fine sable brushes in delicate shades of green and brown, adding gold highlights at the end and the name of each room. By the time she finished, she was light-headed from the heat and the paint fumes, but happy. They were beautiful.

On the way to the paint store, I asked Hugo if we should go back and tape plastic over Lucy's decorations just in case the painters got upstairs before we returned.

No way, he assured me. That hall would take them two full days. Greg said so.

When we got home, I was relieved to see a painter on a towering ladder, hard at work on the ceiling in the downstairs hall. The other assistant wasn't around and Greg's truck was gone, likely to another job they were juggling with ours. I found plastic and masking tape and headed upstairs to cover Lucy's artwork. At the top of the stairs I ran into the second painter, a kid in his teens, with a bucket of primer and a brush in hand, a lit cigarette dangling from his mouth.

"Excuse me, ma'am," he said politely and stood aside. I gasped.

In a surge of efficiency he had gone ahead upstairs to prime the woodwork in the halls, so it could dry and be ready for final enamel the next day. Lucy's work did not escape. Through the thin chalky paint, a ghostly shadow of Lucy's art was visible. Two full days ahead of schedule, the painter had hit all three doors. In tears I went downstairs to find Hugo.

I know it's not a big thing in the overall scheme of the universe, I told him with enraged calm. But I never should have listened to you. This was her gift to us, and the house, and our new life. It represented her presence with us, and it's gone, destroyed.

Hugo asked me to calm down. He'd think of something. The painters, he reminded me, are just kids.

Greg was called and promptly came over. He said the same thing: They're just kids, they didn't know. He and Hugo did not think I should try to repaint her work and pretend it never happened. Tell her the truth, they advised.

I called Lucy and asked her if she knew what a *pentimento* is.

"It sounds like something I ought to know, but don't," she said.

You see it when an artist has a change of mind, I explained. An image is painted over, but the artist's previous idea still shows through. There's a fine example of *pentimento* in Hieronymus Bosch's *Death and the Miser*, a work that asks whether the miser will choose good or evil, angels or demons, when he dies. His empty hand reaches out. Under the thin paint you can see drawing, which shows that the artist originally drew the dying man holding a sack of earthly possessions but then changed his mind. In this way Bosch left the viewer and the miser together to consider what the choice would be, heaven or hell . . .

"What are you trying to tell me?" Lucy interrupted, out of patience.

Your beautiful door decorations, I finally got out. The painter covered them up by accident.

"*What?* Why did he do that?"

It was the clash of two cultures, I think, and everyone in a hurry. Even if the painter had noticed the delicate elm and linden leaves, the luminous, magical-looking acorn, he was probably trying to show the boss how good and quick he was, maybe angling for a raise so he could pay for the truck he needs to get to work. We were in a hurry, too, like animals staking out our territory, to place imprints on the house, make it ours, with a dash of narcissism thrown in. *Look how refined we are, look what nice taste we have.* The house balked, and so did the culture to which it belonged. In a way it was a perfect irony.

"I'm so sorry," I say again. "Do you want me to repaint them?" She hears something in my voice and softens.

"Oh, I'll do it."

Postscript: The following year it was Greg and his painters who bailed Hugo out, when, just before the opening of our second season, he decided to rehab the attic, a grungy cave where wasps and flies and who knew what else lived, a place the housekeeper and even the cat refused to go.

Rushing to finish, Hugo tossed an empty paint can out the third-floor window. The can ricocheted from the side of the house to the ground, and bounced hard. There was more paint in the can than he realized, and it splattered a wide arc of dark teal across the side of the house as high as the second story.

Greg and his crew came the next day and finished covering the dark teal with white before I showed up for the weekend. As I got out of the car, Greg was promising Hugo secrecy. That night Hugo drank a gin and tonic before telling me about it.

CHAPTER
10

Showtime

BY LATE FALL, WHEN THE AREA QUIETS DOWN, THE summer houses close, the big boats sail south for the winter, and some of the restaurants and shops board up, we could see progress everywhere, and smell it.

At last the house's musty, rancid odor yields to the sweet scent of latex paint mixing with breezes gusting in the newly opened windows. Nailed and painted shut for decades, the windows were thoughtfully positioned to catch the slightest stir of air, coming from the bay to the west, the ocean to the east, and the bay and ocean when the wind turned southeast. Clearing northwest winds blew through the utility room, and, if you wanted them, northeasters blustered in the office-bedroom window. Pliers, mallets, screwdrivers, and more than a few broken panes later, you could smell a wind shift. The house has started to breathe.

When I drape the blue-rose fabric across the bay windows in the parlor I know exactly what Mrs. Jefferson would think. *Longer, dearie. I prefer my skirts tea length, if you know what that means these days*. I go out and find the last five yards of the fabric on the remnant table exactly where I'd left it weeks before. It's enough so that the swags reach below the windowsills.

It was a good time. The slog was over and now nothing seemed like too much trouble. Tiredness vanished. I hemmed and hung curtains until after one in the morning and stopped worrying about money because we were close to opening for our first paying guests.

Ethan and Nancy visited for Thanksgiving, tried out the one finished guest room and pronounced it "Fine."

Anything wrong? I pressed. We need to know.

"It's good," Ethan said. "But you need darker curtains, so people can sleep later." I thanked him and silently sighed. Lined curtains are expensive. I decided to wait and see if guests complained.

In early March on a warm rainy afternoon, our third spring at the house, Hugo stopped by The Oaks Inn and told the manager we would be ready for guests next month if they had any overflow. The next day she sent us a booking. It was a bride-to-be and her mother for one night, the first Friday in April.

Miraculous. I wanted to write it down somewhere to make it official but there wasn't a reservation log set up yet or even a notepad around. In the new shed, housing the new furnace, I remembered a wall calendar the propane delivery-man had left. It showed the bright red company truck parked under an enormous oak tree. I found a carpenter's pencil and wrote down the reservation.

No matter that we were playing second fiddle to the other inn—that was the plan. Hugo set the calendar on the table, saying it was time for self-congratulation. Eating dinner that night, we marveled at the reservation and penciled in last-minute tasks to be completed. Even if a dozen things went wrong, I figured, looking at the days left, we would be all set for the first guests.

Around this time a puzzling thing happened. Hugo seemed more anxious every day, even edgy. His mood was moving in inverse relation to our progress. It made no sense. When I reminded him how far we had come, he listed every-thing that was left to do and worried about what was already done and whether it was good enough. He was planning to resand and restain the bedroom floors.

Dust from redoing floors would mean taking down the curtains just hung, rolling up rugs, covering furniture with plastic, taping doors, and it would mean major cleanup after-ward. The windows would have to be rewashed, everything would have to be vacuumed. Even if I covered them, dust would lodge permanently in the brand-new mattresses.

"You must be kidding" was all I could think to say. His nerves weren't the only ones beginning to fray.

Because I couldn't drag a 150-pound sander up and down

the steps or trim a door with the circular saw or do the other heavy work, cleanup was my job. I didn't mind. It seemed like a fair trade-off, although I had heard stories about construction dust wrecking marriages.

Now I got it. Even when I taped doors closed and covered passageways with plastic, dust seeped around—or through?—the plastic and sifted over every surface in the clean, finished rooms on the other side of the house.

I reminded Hugo about this and said that if he started refinishing floors, I was quitting. No, you wouldn't, he said.

Try it and see, I thought. We simply couldn't afford a big step back, like redoing floors, because it would mean too many more months until the third room was ready for paying guests.

In the days leading up to opening weekend, we would be discussing something like this when Hugo would just walk off. It was so unlike him that I followed once to see what he was up to.

Out in the garage he was sawing wood, building something. He didn't want to say what it was because I wouldn't approve.

He picked up a hammer. "It's an enclosure for the electric meter."

Now, when the rooms aren't even finished?

He didn't answer.

I asked if everything was okay.

"Yep." He went back to measuring and sawing.

I suggested that he didn't seem like himself. Was it a reaction to all we'd been through? Or the debt? Should I apologize again for my tantrums along the way? Or was he just decompressing now that the end was in sight?

He didn't think anything was wrong. He felt great about everything, he said and switched on the electric saw.

Five days to go. Hugo wanted to do it really right to prove to the guests, and most of all to himself, that we could.

He moved faster and faster. I could hardly believe how much the painstaking perfectionist could accomplish in a day.

He was moving so fast I never heard about the phone call from his dad, saying Zia Lillia was very ill, until I found him throwing clothes in a knapsack. He planned to drive to Washington, pick up his dad and continue from there straight to New Jersey, where Zia Lillia lived.

That night he called to say she was unable to speak, move, or open her eyes, but she unmistakably squeezed his hand. An hour later she was gone. He sounded hoarse. I asked again if he was all right.

"Not really. Dad kept bugging me to drive faster even though I was already doing seventy-five." He broke off for more news. Home tomorrow to finish details like installing a bedroom door and cleaning up the yard. On Friday he would drive back to New Jersey in time for the funeral on Saturday morning. "So," he concluded, "you'll have to run the bed-and-breakfast."

It wasn't my best moment and I said something like, "What do you mean? This is your business. Why can't the funeral be on Sunday, Monday, Tuesday, Wednesday, or Thursday? The guests will be here on Friday and . . . I have to be in the office on Friday for a very important meeting."

Only one of us had professional catering experience. My experience was limited to working as a waitress at a boardwalk pancake house for a summer and I couldn't even remember if you served from the left and removed from the right or the other way around. My vision for fitting into the new business centered on growing herbs and flowers, baking muffins, discussing the history of our area with guests, and giving them directions to the museums, shops, the best places to kayak, and where to eat crabs on a dock with a sunset view.

I planned to leave everything else to Hugo. His commercial gas range, for one thing, with its 25,000 BTU burners. I knew beyond doubt that it could sense my fear. Then there was the furnace, the pump that ran the well, and a dozen other gadgets that might need adjusting. I didn't even know how to run the credit card machine. This meant crawling under the desk to unplug the phone and disconnect the computer because we didn't have enough outlets and connections to run both, then sitting down on the floor to swipe the card because the machine's cord wasn't long enough to reach the desktop. If the card wouldn't go through, you had to reconnect the phone and call up the credit card company. This wasn't helplessness on my part, it was division of labor. I didn't *want* to know everything.

I could probably handle breakfast, although here was cause for alarm, too, because I had helped with the catering business enough to see that it's one thing to turn out a meal for family and friends but quite another to do it for paying guests. My grandmother's blackberry muffins could be counted on if I didn't forget the baking powder or overbake them, and I had seen Hugo glaze ham in maple syrup and scramble eggs with fresh herbs and butter. But everything would have to be perfect and on time.

Even with his new frenetic pace, Hugo could still be patient and he waited until I had finished talking.

There will be paybacks, he said.

"Like what?" I couldn't think of a payback big enough.

"Big paybacks."

There was promise in his voice, but I saw no reason to let him off easily.

"Well, I'll think about it. But this is the *only* excuse I could possibly accept for you not being here to run *your* business on opening day."

This proved to be the strangest conversation we ever had, though there was no guessing that then. Mumbling a distracted good-night, I was busy considering a payback. One large gift, like a trip, or lots of smaller favors for a long time? The more I considered the second idea, the more I liked it. *Honey, please make me a hot chocolate and while you're up bring me the newspaper and my slippers. Will you stop at the florist on the way home? I'd think I'd like some roses tonight . . .*

CHAPTER
II

April 3

IN THE 1930s FISHERMEN REMOVED THE WEIGHTS AND pulleys from the windows of houses around here to use as weights on their nets. In those hard times our house contributed its share and I pictured one of the big, weightless windows slamming down on the hands of our very first guests. Out in the garage I hunted for a stick to prop the guest bedroom window open. As I yanked one out of a trash can of scrap building materials, a long, thick splinter wedged under my fingernail. It hardly hurt because I was thinking about the lawsuit if a window fell on a guest.

I checked my watch. The guests said they would arrive at 3:30. It was 5:10. They probably weren't coming. They had paid for the night and I wondered if they expected a refund if they couldn't make it. We didn't have a policy about that yet. I found a scrap of sandpaper and started smoothing the wood for another day but stopped when a car hit the driveway hard, spraying gravel up against the fence. Unless it was the tattooed visitor again, it was probably the guests. Someone making a wrong turn would drive more slowly. But what kind of guests?

I smoothed my hair the way my grandmother did when the front doorbell rang and worried what the guests would think if they saw the hostess emerging from a dark garage with a stick in her hand. Weird. I put it down. No, weirder. I picked the wood up to show purpose and walked out.

Coming around the door I saw her, clearly the bride-to-be, pulling suitcases and shopping bags out of a baby-blue sports car. Slipping the stick in my pocket, I greeted her. As a guest, my least favorite part of the bed-and-breakfast experience is arriving and wondering what I've gotten into. If no one's around, the arrival anxiety intensifies. Is the room ready? Is the reservation remembered? Is the host a nutcake? I vowed that we would always go outside to greet guests. Only now I also experienced the other side of it. As host when a guest arrives, I wonder what we've gotten into and if the guest will be a responsible, reasonable person, a nutcake, or worse.

Chic in a starched white shirt, dark capri pants, and slides, she looked worried. She was about the age of my own children. How hard could this be?

"I'm late. Is it okay?"

My chance to be assured. Of course, I told her, your room is waiting.

Relief washed over her face. Without thinking, I offered to help carry her bags. This was supposed to be part of a hospitable welcome and Hugo was supposed to handle it. She pointed to a suitcase that easily weighed forty pounds. With my patched-together knees, there was little possibility I could get it in the house; up the stairs was out of the question. This whole B&B idea was a mistake, I was deciding, when she handed me a shopping bag. I took it gingerly, not wanting to jam the splinter deeper under my nail. In the bag were five shoeboxes. Evidently getting married had changed from the days when all you needed were two pairs of shoes—one for the wedding and one for going away.

"Men are handy to have around, aren't they?" she was saying. I relaxed. She was going to be a good guest.

After three trips from the car with her gear, I showed her the parlor, the dining room, and upstairs.

Fine, she said, explaining that she would be back later with her mother, who was busy with wedding arrangements.

I went back to the garage for the needle-nose pliers and pulled the splinter out.

That night when Hugo called from his aunt's house in New Jersey, I reported every detail of the day.

Up at 5:30 to take care of office work and phone calls. Next, finding something to wear for greeting guests. My sister had anticipated this moment months before and come up with nice gray velvet pants and a black sweater. "I hate it when the hosts look tired and wear old work clothes," she'd said and I had smugly agreed, unaware that they probably were tired and were working when we showed up long before or after the official check-in hours.

I interrupted my account long enough to thank Hugo for stocking the house with food before he left. Then I rushed all day long, I continued. He could not imagine how many last-minute details I expertly attended to. Opening curtains and windows, cleaning windowpanes we had overlooked in our haste, scraping off flecks of paint, finding a hefty wasp building a nest between the screen and the inside of the window at the head of the bed where the guests would sleep. Bug spray didn't faze this wasp in the slightest, so I closed and locked the window. Then I closed the curtains so the guests wouldn't see the wasp. Next, I put flowers and a dish of chocolates in the guest room. I wanted this bed-and-breakfast to be exactly as I expected one to be, inviting, charming, comfortable, and very clean. A good bed-and-breakfast seems effortless, I had noticed, and superior to ordinary surroundings through some magic that ordinary people don't possess.

I looked around and saw paint peelings on the rug, probably from Hugo's last-minute reinstallation of the bedroom door, and vacuumed them up. In their place the vacuum deposited stray threads. I went back and picked them up, but there was nowhere to put them, certainly not in the brand-new guest room wastebasket. I stuck them in the pocket of the velvet pants. Carrying the vacuum cleaner back downstairs, I heard myself hyperventilating.

It was almost three by then, the guests were due any time, and I still had not swept the porch or started getting ready for breakfast. The bride finally arrived, I summed up to Hugo, deciding that it was probably clear to him by now how hard I had worked.

"But all she said when I showed her the room was, 'Fine.'"

"I'm sure it was fine," Hugo said, "and I'm sure you did a fine job. Try to take it easy."

He reported that the family had gathered and everything was set for the funeral. He'd call back at eleven.

When the bride returned with her mother, I said what I had practiced. "We usually serve breakfast at nine, if that's convenient for you." The *we* and the *usually* were intended to give everyone confidence that this was a well-run, experienced establishment and that I wasn't alone and ill at ease, a woman past forty trying on a brand-new role for the first time.

They requested one tea, one coffee, and the bride asked if breakfast could be a little earlier, at 8:30, because she had a lot to do on wedding day.

One tea, one coffee, 8:30, I repeated, going into the kitchen to write it down.

By evening I was setting the round table at the dining room window for their breakfast when I heard rustling behind me. I turned and saw a man sitting on the floor in the parlor. One of the groomsmen, as he introduced himself, he was wrapping gifts. The bride rushed in then and asked where the closest all-night copy store was, because she had to make copies of the wedding programs. I explained that here in the country the closest store, nine miles away, probably closed by six. She said she had left too much for the last minute and the rehearsal dinner wouldn't end until eleven. I looked up the phone number so she could call the store but resisted the impulse to take care of getting the programs copied. Was that part of the job at a really nice bed-and-breakfast?

I spooned jam and butter into small dishes, poured cream into a pitcher, washed tangerines and herbs, filled the sugar bowl, folded napkins, put a spray of flowers on the table, beat the eggs with milk and seasonings, replaced them in the fridge, set out the coffeepot and teapot, and filled the kettle with water. Then I made a sandwich and ate it at our desk. I set two alarm clocks.

Around eleven as I was getting into bed, the phone rang.

"How are they?" Hugo asked.

"What do you mean, how are they?"

"The muffins. Did you make them right, with butter and cream?"

The argument about whose version was better, my original family recipe or the one he developed in cooking school, was longstanding and the more we debated it, the less we agreed. My grandmother made them not sweet by modern standards or buttery, but with a tender batter that holds together more berries than I have ever seen in a single muffin.

When Hugo decided to "improve" the recipe for his catering clients, I did not object. It was cooking school doctrine that lots of butter and cream are essential to give food good "mouth feel" and that fat is a great carrier of flavor. But he went too far when he insisted that guests at a bed-and-breakfast would not want my muffins. Even if his were more cloudlike, which they were, I thought mine tasted more old-fashioned and I intended to use my recipe.

But not now. After a long day, I had no intention of baking any muffins of any kind. "The guests will have to do without."

"But that's what we planned, homemade blackberry muffins. It's supposed to be our signature."

"Don't you have to get some sleep for tomorrow?" I asked before we said curt good-nights.

In an hour the phone rang again. I asked Hugo to hold on while I took the muffins out of the oven. He wanted to know which recipe I used.

"My grandmother's, of course."

"Well, how are they?"

I took my time running a knife around a muffin to loosen it from the pan, tasting, and taking another bite before I picked up the phone again.

"Perfect," I told him.

"Good work," he said. "Have a glass of wine." I said I felt tired in my bones.

Then have a large glass of wine, he suggested.

The next morning the house was silent when I got up before the alarm went off to set plates and cups in the oven to warm. Passing the door between the dining room and the front hall, I spotted a torn piece of lined notebook paper pushed under the door.

CHAPTER
12

April 4

IN THE DIM LIGHT I UNFOLDED THE PAPER AND SAW an almost illegible scribble.

"Back late last night—could we move breakfast to ten?" The innkeeper obviously had something to learn. I went back to the desk and wrote out the guests' bill. With three hours still to go, I made the bed, checked my tax return, signed it, and walked down to the post office.

By 9:30 the fresh juice was squeezed, triangles of thick country bread were ready to be toasted, a basket lined with a napkin waited for the muffins and toast, and condiments were on the table. I switched on the coffeemaker and set the kettle to boil.

Five minutes before ten I opened the dining room door, went into the front hall and listened. It was quiet except for the sound of water running. That was encouraging. The guests were getting ready to come down for breakfast. I opened the front door, went out on the porch, and saw someone hurrying up the road. As she got closer, I recognized the bride, her long hair flying, in jeans and sweatshirt.

Breathless, she came through the gate and up onto the porch. "The bridesmaids and groomsmen are coming over to help put the program together, if that's okay?" I nodded.

After the rehearsal dinner, she explained, she and her friends had driven back across the Bay Bridge to an all-night copy center in Annapolis, the closest place to get two hundred programs copied. All were now impressively stacked on tables in the parlor. The bride started to collate pages, but her hands shook and it took her half a minute to get the first one together and put a paper fastener through the punched-out holes. The program, I saw at a glance, consisted of two different religious ceremonies separated by a jazz concert and ran to eight pages. Two programs assembled a minute, a hundred minutes, I thought, sitting down to help her. She threw me a look that said a thousand thank-yous.

Next, her mother called down the stairs that the towels hadn't been changed since yesterday. Less than twenty-four hours after they arrived, it had not occurred to me to change the towels. This was supposed to be a bed-and-breakfast, after all, and I thought it an unreasonable request. What were they doing with all the new, extra-thick towels anyway? Thinking rude thoughts, I hurried to get her some.

When her mother appeared, I served breakfast while the bridal party assembled programs and the wedding photographer took pictures of everyone. It was 11:40. After serving seconds of coffee and tea, I went into the back room and called Hugo.

"What am I supposed to do now? It looks like they're going to stay all day. Check-out was at eleven." Other innkeepers had warned us that you need to hold your ground because if you make things pleasant enough, some guests just won't leave. It took me a while to get the point and months later, with a group of guests who wanted to linger, I actually made and served five pots of coffee.

Hugo suggested reminding our guests about checkout time and if that didn't work, telling them that new guests are arriving.

I pointed out that no new guests were expected.

"Doesn't matter. Bookings could materialize at any time."

The new life is a sitcom, I told him. Sitting on the floor of my own house in a sea of hole punches, I was collating wedding programs for a complete stranger. Another warning I'd heard, that some bed-and-breakfast owners have trouble sharing their turf—telltale signs are too many rules posted and hosts that seem to be watching the guests around every corner—didn't apply here because we set up as an inn from the beginning. It was just on principle that I thought guests should leave on time. Aside from that, I had to admit it was fun. With the kids far away for school and jobs, it was a relief to be in a house again that reverberated with happy activity, and be part of it. The bride invited me to the wedding.

Back in the dining room, the guests had finished breakfast but showed no sign of getting ready to leave. They seemed to be settling in. I tried dropping a hint by clearing the table, without results. There was nothing to do but approach the bride, now deep in conversation with her mother. I apologized for rushing them, but having a checkout time was to allow us to get ready for the next guests.

It worked. Half an hour later they were gone and I surveyed for damages. They had picked up the hundreds of hole punches and aside from a paper cup of cold coffee in the parlor, the place was spotless. Taking leftover juice, toast, and a cup of coffee to the table, I opened the guest book. I needed comfort to read what, if anything, our first guests thought. I had given my best for Hugo's new business and if it didn't please, it was not for lack of trying.

> *Beautiful house. Can't wait to come back*
> *for the warm hospitality.*

I called up Hugo, who was driving back from New Jersey, and read it to him twice, jubilant because she touched on what I cared about most and thankful that I had kept my mouth shut about the towels and overstaying.

He said he was bringing gifts, rugs, photo albums, silver, and other antiques. More would arrive next week by moving van.

Very nice, I said, but I was thinking about a trip or a series of favors or—I suddenly knew what the payback would be.

We ate Italian food and discussed it while eating. We listened to Caruso and Pavarotti at Sunday dinner. A trip always meant Italy. All delightful, but as the novelty of marrying into an Italian family wore off, I began to miss my own family traditions and yearned to revisit them before they faded to vague or forgotten memories.

The payback was equal time for my heritage. A visit to the farm at Antietam and the little Dunker church where my great-great-grandfather had preached the evening before the Civil War battle. I also wanted to see the gravesite of my half-Indian ancestor and the Seneca lands in New York State. This ancestry represented an unspeakable embarrassment to my German-Huguenot family and was never discussed. In a neatly typed family history, a tiny, cramped hand noted the fact as an afterthought. We would visit Antietam and Seneca territory and we would start cooking and eating American Indian foods.

Hugo agreed to consider the idea more after the upcoming, fully booked weekend at the bed-and-breakfast. In two weeks, all three rooms were reserved for the first time and for two nights. These bookings also came from The Oaks, which was hosting another wedding. Six room nights in the lingo, a big step up. Twelve breakfasts and twelve teas to plan, cook, and serve. The third room was almost ready.

With ten days to go until the big weekend and with two more bookings before that, I decided to go away. This would allow Hugo to experience running the place by himself as I had, and would help him understand it better. I missed Lucy and Amanda and it was my only chance of seeing them anytime soon. So the plan was only half revenge.

Returning from the all-girls holiday, Hugo met me at the airport. "It was a lot of work, running the B&B without you." He picked up my suitcase.

Tell me all about it, I said, giving him a light kiss.

Listening just enough to gather that all went well with a couple and a single lady who had stayed, I gazed out the truck window at the wide, green fields and lines of oaks, pines, and flowering pear as we approached the Chesapeake Bay Bridge and the Eastern Shore. I missed Amanda and Lucy, but with

Hugo beside me and the clean, grassy fragrance of springtime fields mixing with the briny breezes, I felt something almost like coming home.

Home. A complicated concept. A bed-and-breakfast done right is an idealized kind of home, more homey somehow than a real one. We evidently had gotten that part right. But a true home for us, I had to admit, seemed stubbornly elusive, quite imaginable but not exactly within reach.

Hugo was still listing everything that needed doing as we pulled into the driveway. The door to the secret back-stairs, which would be used for the first time by guests staying in the small, romantic room at the top of those stairs, needed work. This rickety handmade door was definitely quaint, but the peeling brown paint, which showered chips all over the landing when the door opened or closed and the wind blew around like confetti, definitely was not. The door needed scraping, filling, sanding, and painting. If there was time, the battered wooden stairs needed the same. We started in.

By dusk, both door and stairs were ready for under-coating. Hugo disappeared into the kitchen and I heard the uplifting clink of ice against glass—grown-ups' school bell. Workday's over. We walked outside, past tools, paint buckets, ladders, and refuse, to the lawn. From here you could look out to Oak Creek and see lights coming on. A party was in progress somewhere. A jazz group started up.

Stars came out. A wispy breeze drifted off the creek. Behind us the house in its new white paint glowed in the afterlight of the day. Hugo took my hand and we did an easy two-step.

It lasted less than five minutes, but for once I made a point of noticing, and memorizing the moment. The house with its promise of a new life, the grass, the breeze, the music, us dancing. A time of perfect happiness that nothing could ever take away.

13

Undertoad

A BRIGHT, ENERGIZING MID-MAY MORNING. WE MADE a quick trip to the Western Shore so Hugo could buy last-minute supplies and I could keep a doctor's appointment. The office headaches were getting worse, although they rarely struck on weekends when I was at the bed-and-breakfast. The doctor thought environmental factors might be responsible and tried tests, diet, medications. Nothing helped. He ruled out a brain tumor because brain tumors, he said, don't clear up on weekends. After the appointment, I did office work at our house which still served as base camp until we would move full time to the bed-and-breakfast.

Hugo set out around two-thirty that afternoon for the Eastern Shore, late considering all that needed doing in forty-eight hours. Before he left I stood in the driveway next to his truck, where he sat ready to start the engine. We congratulated each other on being really prepared to run a bed-and-breakfast. Each of us had done it alone. This could only be easy. It represented the culmination of all the dreams and work, all the past disappointments set aside, the curtain rising on a brand-new life. Apparently, the stresses hadn't even dented our marriage. They might have had an opposite effect, Hugo pointed out as he leaned back on the truck seat to catch the sunlight on his face, because this start-a-new-life-on-a-shoestring business was too fragile to survive serious disagreement—and we both knew it.

Little fights were allowed and we took a minute to replay the one about the color for the front door. I had chosen grass-green, as described by Mr. Don Harper, whose family opened the Pasadena Inn across the street in 1902 and he grew up there. A centenarian when I met him at a summer picnic, Mr. Harper said the front door and shutters of our house were always green with cherry red trim on the window sashes.

Wanting to evoke bay surroundings, Hugo insisted on maritime blue. When I consented to blue to make peace and sanded, primed, and painted the door with two glossy coats of a color called Welcome Blue and it turned out not to be the blue he saw in his mind's eye, this caused almost as much trouble as the blackberry muffins. Hugo glanced at his watch. Time was up.

His to-do list for Thursday and Friday was taped to the dashboard:

1. Mow lawn

2. Backstairs, final blue paint & do ahead so no fumes

3. Plane sticking front door

4. Clean up junk, gravel, mulch, 2-x-4s, bags cement

5. Lay timbers in driveway so guests know where to park

6. Test cream waffle recipe for Sunday

7. *Food shop, two breakfasts, two teas*
8. *Buy guest soaps, shampoos etc.*
9. *Laundry!!*

Everyone who's "been there" warns that the worst part of running a bed-and-breakfast is the laundry. You can't run the washer and dryer when guests are in our house or out on the lawn because it might interfere with the bucolic serenity they expect. But in a small bed-and-breakfast it's only a problem, I discovered, if you fall behind. Naturally, we were behind after only two weeks. With laundry stacked on the desk and bed, there was nowhere to eat, sleep, or pay bills. We weren't even close to having the housekeeping help we promised ourselves once the business picked up. So Hugo planned to get right on it.

My plan called for finishing up the week at the office and arriving Friday night, after Hugo checked in the guests and served the first afternoon tea. I would help out on Saturday and Sunday.

When I'm working and need to concentrate, I usually let the phone ring and return calls later. Maybe this time I needed a break. When the phone rang, I answered.

No one seemed to be on the line.

As I started to hang up, a rasp came from the phone. I couldn't be sure. It sounded like Hugo and it didn't sound like him. I had never heard this voice before and went cold. The undertoad, I thought, the unexpected thing John Irving called it, that always gets you when you're looking the other way.

"What's up?" I asked. "Where are you?"

"Sick," he said.

I thought it must be an accident because he was never sick.

"Are you in the truck?"

"Can't talk . . ."

"Where are you?"

"Fifty."

"Route 50?"

"Yes."

"Where on Route 50?"

"Can't see . . ."

"You have to see. Look, and tell me where you are."

He said something about Hess Road. I vaguely remembered an exit from Route 50. Did he mean that? Yes, he said.

I told him to call 911 while I called them, too. Minutes later when I called him back, his phone clicked on and I heard a siren.

"They're here" was all he said.

The siren got loud and I heard walkie-talkies and voices, but I couldn't make out what they were saying.

The Upside Down

A 52-YEAR-OLD GENTLEMAN WAS DRIVING TO HIS BED-and-breakfast on the Eastern Shore . . . I didn't want there to be more and the words kept rerunning when I tried to read the report later. *A gentleman was driving to his bed-and-breakfast . . . and everyone lived happily ever after.*

Four o'clock, a weekday, rush hour. The roads would be jammed for three more hours. I started locking doors and windows, switching off lights. Call the cat sitter, a small methodical part of myself directed, say you don't know when you'll be back. Pack. Don't forget the muffin recipe. I slipped the index card with my grandmother's faded script in my shirt pocket.

What else? Linens for the third guest room, also a lamp and a crocheted tablecloth that would do for a bedskirt. Bedskirt? How could I even be thinking about a bedskirt at a time like this? What time this was I couldn't say. There was fear in my throat and eyes. Something was horribly wrong.

What next? Call the hospital in Easton where they would be likely to take someone who was injured on the highway— unless it was a helicopter evacuation to a big medical center. But where would that be? I had no idea. I called the hospital and identified Hugo, his truck, the time of the rescue.

They connected me right away to the emergency room and a cardiologist came on the line. One of the upper chambers of Hugo's heart started beating uncontrollably, he explained. Not a heart attack. They were giving him medicine.

He's stable, the cardiologist said. "But we haven't got the fibrillation stopped so he's going to be here a while." The cardiologist was clearly smart and experienced. He answered my questions before I could ask.

"There are other things we'll try," he said. "This by itself isn't life-threatening but it can cause blood clots, so we're giving him medicines to prevent that. His vital signs are good."

Vital signs? My young, strong husband was between life and death with doctors watching his vital signs. If it did not seem so unlikely I would have been much more upset. I dialed Hugo's dad.

As the phone rang, I realized it would be important to go easy. A medical man or not, he was almost ninety. My casual greeting didn't work.

"What's up, Carol?"

There's a problem, I said, but everything's going to be fine. I wanted to let him know that Hugo wasn't feeling well and he was, just for now, in the hospital.

"What's he got?"

Atrial fibrillation.

"Jesus!"

I had never heard him invoke a deity, and asked if it was bad.

It can be or not, he said. He would get some information and call back.

By the time I sped across the Bay Bridge it was dark. Slowing down at Hess Road, I spotted Hugo's silver-gray pickup parked just off the highway in tall grass. This will turn out to be nothing, I decided, seeing that his truck was neatly parallel to the guard-rail. He couldn't be very sick or he would have crashed into the rail. When I get to the hospital he'll be gone, he will have checked out. I will go to the B&B and he'll be there waiting for me.

I didn't exactly know where the hospital was, even though I had been in the pin-neat, picturesque county seat of Easton, a dozen miles from our village, before. There was no one out on the streets walking or driving, an unfamiliar sight to a city dweller. I stopped at a gas station for directions.

When the attendant said, "Straight ahead on your right, ma'am," I wanted to hug him. The *ma'am* meant more than he would know. It meant that you and where you are going deserve courtesy, you are not a lost soul driving through the dark, alone without family or friends, to an unknown situation in a strange town.

The hospital looked dark and closed up. Two doors I tried were locked. I walked around to the emergency entrance, where a guard let me in. I signed the log and followed directions up to the second floor.

Three intravenous lines extended from each of Hugo's arms and bleeping monitors were attached all over his chest. A wall of machines behind him blinked green, blue, and white. His eyes were closed.

I said his name and touched his arm.

Hey, he said without opening his eyes.

I couldn't think of what to do except hold his hand. He didn't need or want anything. I topped off his water pitcher and refolded the blanket on his bed. The nurse said they would keep a close eye on him overnight and the doctors would come by early in the morning. Hugo could hardly speak, but agreed when I brought up the idea of leaving to get ready for the guests. In a small town if we disappointed the guests, word would spread and no one could be expected to refer any more business our way.

It was after midnight and very dark without streetlights or a moon as I headed out Route 33, the only car on the road. Past the Three Sisters Café, closed, I turned onto Ditch Road, so-called because of the deep drainage ditches on both sides, and drove slowly, carefully past Big Woods, past the Woman Tree so named for its suggestive branching. It wouldn't do to get stuck in a ditch right now.

In the driveway it was even darker. By the car headlights, I made my way up the path and unlocked the kitchen door. Swarming mosquitoes trailed me into the house.

Switching on the light in the "office," the twelve-by-fourteen-foot owners' quarters, I saw white mountains of towels, sheets, table mats, and napkins piled on the sofa bed and desk and spilling onto the floor, blocking my way. *No crying over laundry, please,* I could hear Zia Lillia say, and smiled in spite of myself. What a surprise to find her here.

There was no choice. I started on the laundry. The laundry room was still jammed with ladders, paint cans, and lumber, some too heavy for me to move. I stacked the ladders to one side, clearing a narrow path, and put in the first load before I fell asleep on the sofa.

Check-in time was clearly stated on our reservation confirmations as four to six o'clock, but Hugo had told me that while I was away, the guests showed up at eleven in the morning. Sometimes they just do what they want to do, he said, just like us when we're traveling. The early guests arrived off a red-eye flight from California and he felt he had to let them in, offer tea and a bite to eat, even though lunch and dinner aren't part of the bed-and-breakfast deal. He concluded that you have to be ready early.

I remembered my grandmother's expression, "Work backward," meaning in this situation shop and ready the rooms before doing anything else. Seeing Hugo and talking with the doctors would have to wait . . .

Your desperately ill husband will have to wait? I wondered if I was thinking straight. Hospitalized patients often need an advocate to look after them, speak up, and generally help out. But if I canceled the rooms out from under the guests, ruining the new business on account of him, his spirit might be crushed. There was a lot riding on this project.

As I was considering what to do that morning, Hugo's dad called. He had talked with the cardiologist, who said Hugo was going to be fine and would probably be discharged today or tomorrow. My spirits lifted. With that news, I decided to go ahead with the arriving guests.

On top of everything else, the grass was ankle-high along the driveway, overdue for mowing. Hugo's approach to the lawn was Zen-like. With his push-mower, it took most of a day to cut the lawn and he liked it that way. I called up the Kilmons to ask if they knew anyone who could help.

Scott answered the phone and I told him what had happened the day before to Hugo. Barely had I formed the question about the grass when he said, "It's taken care of." I wanted to cry. He went on to say that Susie would come over and give me a hand. She could cook, make beds, anything at all I needed. I knew she had a bad back and couldn't bring myself to ask her to do beds or wait on tables. "We're here if you change your mind," he said. I should have accepted, but being new, I felt awkward asking favors of them.

It was one of those times when everyone who might have helped was not around. Rick, away on a business trip. My two best friends, out of town for the weekend. Linda, in Florida to check on our ninety-two-year-old mother. Ethan, Lucy, and Amanda, thousands of miles away at work and school. I knew I could turn out breakfast under the circumstances, but I also knew I couldn't serve it graciously or even calmly.

I called up a server at our favorite eating place in Easton, where we allowed ourselves to go once a week when we didn't have a kitchen. Amy Haines, the restaurant's owner who was by now a friend, had told me we could raid her staff if necessary, but only for weekend mornings. The server said she would be glad to come over. By phone my sister suggested keeping the menu simple.

I called the hospital. Hugo answered and told me not to worry, he felt a little better and there were a lot of doctors around. He wanted to know if his truck was okay.

Fine, I assured him. He said something else then, so softly it took time for his words to register. "In the fast lane . . . doing seventy . . . and the yellow line . . ."

What yellow line?

The one in the middle of the highway, he explained. "Upside down . . . it seemed to be in the sky . . . and I was driving with the truck . . . on its side."

New panic washed over me. I rushed through the work to get more or less ready for the incoming guests and drove as fast as I dared back along Ditch Road, heading for the hospital.

When I arrived, Hugo was still lying in bed, too dizzy to sit up or open his eyes.

Full House

FRIDAY NOON. WHEN I ANSWERED THE PHONE, A WOMAN asked for Hugo. He isn't here, I told her.

"Oh. This is Kayla and I just wanted to let Hugo know we've landed so we'll be at his place by three."

His place? This was a courteous guest, even if she seemed quite focused on Hugo. I thanked her for calling and remembered to say something welcoming.

A few minutes after three, a couple parked and walked up the brick path, presumably Kayla and her husband. But who knew? You can't be sure who the guests are until they identify themselves. For this reason I quickly got in the habit of introducing myself to encourage them to do the same.

"Hi, I'm me," the man responded. Kayla stepped forward and introduced herself and Bob, her husband. I offered to help carry their bags but, having learned from before, asked if they had something light because of a knee.

"Looks to me like you've got two knees," Bob said, handing me a bag of cookies and soda. "It's in case you don't have much to eat around here."

He's more comfortable with hotels, Kayla said, but he agreed to try a bed-and-breakfast. I showed them to their room and Kayla asked if Hugo was around.

"What's all this about Hugo?" Bob said. "She's called him three times in the last three days. I asked her why she had to call Hugo again from the airport. Is she in love with him or something?"

He tends to have that effect, I said.

"Then we'll look forward to meeting him," Bob said with a wink.

Coming downstairs for tea, Kayla and Bob carried a bottle of wine they had brought from California. I thanked them for the completely unexpected gift and said I'd save it for when Hugo could enjoy it.

Teatime passed quickly. I felt a rush of delight at meeting such a pleasant couple, people I just knew Hugo would take to. Alone back in the kitchen to refill the teapot, the bleak reality hit me. Hugo was lying in a hospital bed and couldn't get up. No one knew what was wrong with him. Maybe he would never be able to taste the wine. He loved wine and would talk about the grapes, the regions, the variations from one vineyard to another. I would rather not drink the wine at all than drink it without him, even with the annoying slurping noises of his first sips. This is necessary to aerate wine properly, he said, and the only way to experience the full taste. I blinked back tears and pushed through to the dining room. Luckily, Kayla kept up the conversation, complimenting details of the house restoration and decoration I didn't think anyone would notice while Bob interrupted with jokes. Pride kept me going, too. No one wants to see a crying hostess.

"Bob doesn't usually like inns, but he likes this," Kayla was saying. "However, we will need more pillows, I can tell you that right now, at least two more."

Certainly, I said, knowing there wasn't an extra pillow in the house and the closest store was a sixteen-mile trip.

The doorbell rang and I went to greet the guests for the second room, a stately gray-haired couple. I ran through information about the house, already easier the second time in a day. Here's the parlor for your use, the dining room where we serve breakfast at nine and tea in the afternoon, or you can have tea on the porch. Here are the keys, and up these stairs straight ahead is your room.

One tea, one coffee for the Linden room, I repeated, coming back downstairs. I had forgotten to ask Kayla and Bob about coffee and tea, but found them on their way out for the evening. As I was writing down the requests, a third car pulled into the driveway and parked. I went out to greet a woman alone.

She had encountered Bob outside.

"What's with the 'I'm-me' jokester?" she asked sharply.

Mediating between guests, it crossed my mind for the first time, might be part of the job and it might not be easy. I followed this guest into the house and showed her around.

My head was spinning as I anxiously jotted down "coffee, Acorn," afraid of forgetting even this simple detail. She reappeared half an hour later, ready to join a wedding rehearsal party, and paused at the kitchen door.

"May I make a suggestion?"

"Yes, of course." But if you don't like this place, please don't say so now, I thought, because my husband might be dying and I am about to start screaming.

"Lights. I've stayed in a lot of B&Bs. I'm something of an authority on them, by the way, and I don't know why everyone thinks no one reads in bed! I have moved the reading light from the table to the bedside. Will you please be sure that no one moves it back when they do my room?"

Yes, I answered, completely missing her main point. I was listening only for immediate problems.

"And another thing—pillows. If you are going to have shams, and they're nice ones by the way, then you must also provide pillows with pillowcases on them. I'll need two. You cannot expect your guests to take the pillows out of the shams."

Pillows again. I was starting to perceive a trend.

"Of course," I said, knowing the local department store was by now closed for the night. There was a superstore farther away. If they were open late, maybe I could buy pillows there on my way back from seeing Hugo.

The Acorn guest was saying something else. When it sank in, I panicked. She promised "additional comments" at breakfast. Even in my distracted state I realized that this could only mean one thing. She was planning to embarrass me and our little business in front of the other guests. If she did that, there was a good chance I'd lose it. Running a bed-and-breakfast suddenly seemed like an extremely bad idea. You have to remain calm, cool, resilient, and flexible, other owners had advised, also helpful and cheerful. I hadn't paid enough attention at the time, thinking yes, yes, I know all that. I never stopped to consider the implications. You have to be like that, even if your own life is falling apart.

When Hugo and I talked later on the phone, I told him about the nice guests and the lovely North Coast wine waiting for him. I told him everything was organized and going smoothly.

The next morning, Saturday, I got up early and went into the kitchen. As before, I had done most of the work for breakfast the night before while the guests were out. Now with a guest for the first time sleeping in the room directly over the kitchen, I had to move quietly, which took extra time. When I set a pan on the stainless steel counter, the sound bounced off the ceiling. I washed the tangerines and sliced them for juicing, but set them aside because the juicer sounded like a lawnmower. I boiled water for tea, started the coffeemaker. At 7:30 I walked into the dining room to set the tables. Through the glass doors to the parlor, I was startled to see Bob sitting on the sofa, arms crossed, obviously waiting for someone or something.

I waved and hoped he didn't notice my worn-out moccasins as I opened the doors. I attempted a serene greeting.

"Morning. Could I possibly have a cup of tea? Earl Grey, please."

He was testing the place. I knew we didn't have any Earl Grey, but maybe Lady Grey.

"Fine, Lady Grey," he laughed. "Let's try her out, and a newspaper if you have one?"

"Certainly," I said, having completely forgotten this detail. Minutes later, as Melanie came up the walk, I dashed out and whispered to her to get a paper. As I was serving Bob his second cup of tea, she returned with it. Breakfast was behind schedule by now and he still wanted to chat. I knew that with Melanie's help I could pull everything together quickly, so I decided to visit with him for another ten minutes.

Frankly, he didn't care at all for B&Bs. As a commercial airline pilot, he liked hotel services. This time Kayla insisted and he had to admit he felt right at home here. But could he make a suggestion?

I was starting to expect this. So what if I'd stayed in over a hundred bed-and-breakfasts and thought I knew all about the business?

Whatever it was would be interesting, maybe something to learn from. Of course, I said.

"Light from your sign. It shines on the ceiling in our room. Anything you can do about that?"

After the electrician installed these lights, I'd noticed the problem, but the electrician couldn't come back for another week. I told Bob I would look into it, knowing I didn't have a clue how to fix it. Hugo had said something about it earlier and maybe he would be well enough today to remember. Bob would know exactly how to do it, but I couldn't bring myself to ask a guest for help.

At nine o'clock everyone gathered in the dining room. Kayla and Bob chose the round table by the front window. The couple from the Linden room sat at the large center table, and I set a place for the Acorn guest at a small table at the other end of the room. The idea was to allow the guests privacy if they wanted it or the opportunity to socialize if they preferred. I was happy when the Linden couple asked if the Acorn guest would like to join them and she quickly agreed. I moved her place setting over to their table.

Fresh tangerine juice in the little glasses Hugo had specially chosen for that purpose was already set on the tables, along with baskets of toast and muffins. Melanie came out and poured coffee and tea. Never let guests sit at the table without anything to eat or drink, Hugo had lectured, and I told Melanie back in the kitchen that he would be proud of how we were doing.

It took only a few minutes to scramble the eggs and decorate each plate with fresh thyme and roasted tomatoes. As Melanie opened the dining room door and carried in plates, I overheard animated conversation.

Turning off the stove, I brought out the last two breakfasts while Melanie refilled coffee cups. The Acorn guest had been talking, but I didn't catch what she was saying. The dining room fell silent.

Then Kayla said, "You can have our blanket."

"You can have ours, too," the lady from Linden spoke up. Quietly but distinctly she added, "I have my husband to keep me warm."

The Acorn guest eyed me. "You forgot to put salt and pepper on the table."

"Right here." I hurried to set Zia Lillia's little crystal salt and pepper shakers down and retreated to the kitchen.

What were they saying? I asked Melanie who came in a minute later. She threw me a look that was both sympathetic and evasive. "Oh, that lady's just a complainer. But they really like the breakfast—all of them."

Heartened, I returned to the dining room to ask if all was well.

"The bed was good," Acorn said, "but I'd like more juice."

After making and pouring more juice and coffee, I described some of the local sights and restaurants. Within an hour all the guests went out.

Melanie helped put the kitchen back in order before leaving. I straightened sofa cushions in the parlor, folded the newspaper, swept the porch, took an extra blanket upstairs and left it outside Acorn's door.

After returning phone calls from worried family, I made tea, carried it into the office, and bolted the door. I switched off the lights and sat down on the bed. A migraine was setting in fast. I sipped a little tea. As soon as I lay down, someone rapped sharply at the door. I sat up and heard the Acorn guest calling my name.

Insistently the doorknob turned. I flung myself out of bed. Fortunately, the lock held because our living quarters, a confusion of power tools, laundry, paperwork, suitcases, and dirty dishes, would have shocked anyone who saw it except other bed-and-breakfast owners who mostly say they lived in similar conditions while getting their places going.

"Carol?" she called again.

I opened the door and stepped into the hall, closing the door quickly behind me. Dressed and perfumed for the wedding, she looked very displeased.

"They haven't made up my room yet."

"That's not . . . I mean, we consider the room yours while you're here and we don't go in unless asked."

"It's quite a mess," she said.

Worrisome as that was, I considered apologizing to her, but now stress was taking its toll and I didn't want to apologize. Some bed-and-breakfasts offer daily maid service, but many do not and we thought this style more suited short-stay visitors to our small place.

I brought myself to say that I would go see what the problem was.

"Please," she said and was gone.

I called up Hugo. Always the more easygoing of our team, he managed to offer sympathy while suggesting that it wouldn't be hard to take a look around, make a bed if necessary. If she had made a "mess," better to find out now.

I took the duplicate key and clean towels and went upstairs. Outside her door the extra blanket was where I had left it. In the room the normal kinds of things were lying around, a book and clothes, tourist brochures. The bathroom was another story. Wet towels and the rug were heaped on the floor next to a wastebasket overflowing with soda cans, a partly eaten pizza, candy wrappers, plastic bags, and a wine bottle. Thinking it probably wasn't easy in late middle age to travel alone to a wedding, I replaced the towels, collected the trash, made her bed, took the extra blanket out of its bag and laid it out in neat accordian folds at the foot of the bed, the way they do at luxury hotels so you can pull the blanket up and it slides gently over you.

In my dreams of our new life, there wasn't anything about being a housemaid. When I called Hugo back to complain about this part of the dream, he sounded brighter. This is only while we get started, he reminded me. Once we're successful we'll have some help.

By late Saturday afternoon when I got to the hospital, he was sitting up, although one side of his body seemed stiff, as if he was partly paralyzed. I knew he was trying to put on a good show by sitting up, but his closed eyes gave him away. Yes, he admitted, his head hurt like hell.

The cardiologist stood next to the bed, clearly unhappy. "The medicine isn't working," he said. "Here we have a relatively young patient, healthy until three days ago, who now can't even drive himself home from the hospital." He had consulted the neurologist and ordered more tests. Results tomorrow.

When he left, I gave Hugo the strawberries I had brought. He half-opened his eyes and started eating, then stopped. He almost forgot: His dad said to call right away. It was critical.

The Experts

ON THE OTHER END OF THE LINE, HUGO SENIOR ordered me to hold my index finger in front of Hugo's nose and move it to the right and then the left. Phone in hand, I climbed up on the hospital bed, sat cross-legged in front of Hugo, and told him to look at my finger.

"Does his right eye follow your finger when you move to his right?" his dad wanted to know. I tried it twice before saying yes. Then he asked me to do the same with his left eye. "Start at his nose and move your finger to his left, your right. Does his eye make a jerky motion?"

Yes.

"Jesus!"

What does that mean? I asked. He answered by instructing me to try it again.

As his eye moved from center to right, following my finger, I watched closely. There was no mistake. His blue-green eye tried to follow my finger with tiny, flickering hesitations.

"Jesus Christ!"

I asked him again what it meant. Stroke.

Hugo wanted to know what his dad was saying. I told him calmly because I didn't really believe it and because he seemed a little better than before.

At the same time his dad was directing me to get the neurologist on the phone *immediately* and get the results of the latest test, an MRI of the head.

He's not on call, the hospital operator advised and gave me his office number. An answering machine came on, saying to leave a message for Monday or to call the hospital. He could be bleeding into his head, I kept thinking, not knowing if a stroke could cause that, but vaguely remembering something about it and that it could be fatal. I went to find a nurse.

"It is Saturday night, you know," the nurse on duty said. "Normally, the doctors aren't in the hospital at this time." I told her we had to find out the results of the MRI immediately. She checked the files. There was no record of the afternoon's test results. I was hyperventilating again. She agreed to call the neurologist.

Ten minutes later she handed the phone to me. For the first time I broke down. He waited patiently until I stopped crying, identified myself, and said Hugo's dad, a retired neurosurgeon, thought Hugo had a stroke and we thought he was bleeding into his head and didn't know what to do.

Fifteen minutes after that, the area's only neurologist, in blue jeans, flannel shirt, and cowboy hat, came in and sat down. Resting one booted foot on the hospital bed, he tipped back his hat and looked at me. "He's not bleeding into his head, so you don't have to worry about that." He turned to Hugo then, lying down, eyes closed.

"How old are you?"

Fifty-two, Hugo told him. He flipped through Hugo's chart.

"Well, you fucked up big time, my friend."

At that Hugo opened his eyes and stared at the doctor with interest.

"What are we going to do with you?" the doctor went on. "You've had a stroke, a BIG one."

He let that sink in. I held my breath.

"I'll tell you what's going to happen. Your life is going to change, buddy. Diet—low fat, low salt—and medications, lots of them, for the rest of your life. But you're going to be okay. You're going to get better and walk out of here. You're damn lucky the stroke was on the left side."

He turned back to me. "Tell his dad to relax. Hugo is not bleeding into his brain. There is no dangerous swelling. There are signs that he had a stroke. Tell his dad that from now on Hugo will need an internist and a cardiologist, but he isn't going to need any neurosurgeon."

Hugo was wide awake, observing the doctor intently, and I saw light in his eyes again.

Your problem, the doctor continued, was undiagnosed high blood pressure and high cholesterol. No, I confessed, Hugo did not have an internist. His internist had retired about ten years back and we'd been too busy to find a new one.

The neurologist raised an eyebrow and listed the eleven medications Hugo would take. As soon as he felt better and could walk as far as the nurses' station, he could go home. He closed the chart.

"You're Western Shore?"

Hugo nodded.

"Like it here?"

"Yes, until now," Hugo said.

"Western Shore . . ." He shook his head. "Except for a medical meeting, I haven't crossed over in twenty years." He stood up, tipped his hat and was gone.

Hugo reminded me that someone had to take care of the guests and I ought to get going too. He told me how to fix the spotlight that was keeping the airline pilot awake. Take a Phillips screwdriver, loosen a screw hidden below the base of the light, rotate the light, and retighten the screw.

Overjoyed with the good news, I hugged Hugo, headed off to the superstore five miles farther away to buy pillows and pillowcases and from there to the market. For Sunday morning I planned apple-sour cherry crisp with whipped cream, flavored with Rebel Yell for an Eastern Shore touch, along with sausage and toast.

It was late again by the time I got back with the food and nine fluffy, oversized pillows, because I never wanted to hear about pillows again, and distributed three to each room. With a flashlight I went out front and fixed the spotlight.

By now some of the guests were back from the wedding, I saw by lights in the upstairs windows. In the kitchen when I started whisking the cream in a metal bowl, in the silent house in the silent countryside without any cars or planes passing by, it crashed and echoed around like timpani. I carried the mixing bowl, whisk, and bourbon into the office, but now I was directly below the Acorn guest's bed. Gathering everything up, I went into the bathroom, set the bowl on a dish towel in the tub, and knelt down to whip the cream. The sound of metal against metal bouncing off the porcelain echoed even louder than before. When I tried draping a towel over the bowl, the whisk got tangled in the towel.

I gave up, put the cream back in the fridge, brought the Rebel Yell into the office, lay down on the unmade bed and took a drink. I started laughing, then crying.

The phone rang. *Jesus, I don't even get to cry.* It might be the hospital. I sat up and blew my nose. I took a breath and tried to answer evenly. There might be important news about Hugo, a decision to be made.

You don't sound like yourself, my sister said. "I'm fine," I lied before giving in completely. "I'm too upset to run the business."

"Of course you can and you are," Linda said calmly. She asked about Hugo and about what was planned for Sunday breakfast. Then over the phone her voice dropped to the one I remembered from childhood when we lay next to each other in our double bed sharing secrets and reassurances. "Just think," she said now in that long-ago voice, "after this, nothing about this business will ever be hard again."

17

Sunday Morning

IN THE KITCHEN MELANIE POURED TWO MUGS OF COFFEE while we waited for the guests to show up. Breakfast was all ready, the warm apple-cherry crisp with bourbon whipped cream and country sausages browned to a turn. A tap on the kitchen door startled me and through the screen I saw Julie. I opened the door and she gave me a hug. "Was the grass cut all right?" she asked. Jerry, her husband, had done it in a rush because it was a peak season for his landscaping business. More than perfect, I assured her.

On Sundays her antiques shops didn't open until eleven, so she came over to help serve breakfast. I hugged her back and pointed to Melanie in the kitchen, promising to call if I needed anything. As Julie left, I shook my head. The busiest people always made time for others.

Back in the house, I put on baroque guitar music softly and opened the dining room doors. Immediately I sensed something different.

As the guests sat down, I poured coffee and tea.

"Everything is just wonderful, we slept so well!" Kayla greeted me.

"Yes, excellent!" Bob added.

The lady from the Linden room spoke up. "It was perfectly warm and comfortable. We didn't need any blanket."

"Neither did we," Kayla said and the two couples launched into conversation. If the Acorn guest had a complaint, she couldn't have gotten in a word. Although Acorn had requested just coffee because of a wedding brunch, I set out fruit and toast for her and she thanked me, twice.

Bob wanted me to sit down at their table to visit.

How much should a host socialize? Socializing is a big part of why people love or hate the bed-and-breakfast experience. My concept was to let the guests decide. The house party approach, with the guests all sitting together at a big table and being expected to carry on bright, sociable conversation early in the day with each other, and usually with the host as well, was once more or less standard. I never liked it and was relieved to find that, according to recent market research, most guests don't either.

Now guests were inviting me to join them, but I couldn't be sure if they were just being polite, doing the expected thing. I had met an ideal bed-and-breakfast host years before, a retired college president who had mastered the role. He made two efficient, scintillating appearances of about ten minutes each, at breakfast and teatime. In the morning he answered questions about guests' plans for the day and offered ideas about activities, sightseeing, and local politics and culture. "Did you happen to notice all those billboards along the causeway to the island—hundreds of them?" I remembered him saying. "You probably wonder how they got there." Everyone did and he told the story, which provided a revealing glimpse of this small Virginia town's power politics.

At teatime, when dinner menus from local restaurants came out, he really shone, delivering witty, informed critiques that all began with, "The best thing they do—" As in, "The best thing they do is an extraordinary bouillabaisse with fresh local oysters, if you don't mind a décor of fishnets and plastic lampshades." And: "The best thing the place across the street does is a pear-endive salad, if you want to pay $17 for it. Of course you can get that very same salad down the way for a quarter the price."

He helped you understand a place from the inside out and then he was gone. Perfect, I noted at the time, because you always learned something worthwhile from him that you wouldn't find in a guidebook and he always left you looking forward to his next appearance. The rest of the time you were free to imagine that his house was yours, a romantic fantasy that is supposed to be a central part of bed-and-breakfast charm. This is all yours without any work!

Now I, who scorned the intrusive host, often the only flaw in a perfect bed-and-breakfast stay, was considering sitting down with the guests. If they brought it up again, I decided to make it short. Melanie garnished the plates and I carried them out, explaining that the Rebel Yell was a local custom. Kayla insisted that I sit down and Bob pulled another chair up to their table. I poured myself a cup of coffee and joined them.

Kayla asked how Hugo was and I told her a little better. She squeezed my hand, intuiting that more was wrong than I'd said. Bob reiterated praise for the house, the ambience, and the comfort. Then Bob, Kayla, and the Linden guests took turns asking me about the history of the house and the business itself. Like my ideal host, I tried to give short, insightful answers and looked for a way to turn the conversation in their direction.

At the first opportunity I asked Bob if I might ask him a question. He seemed amused.

What would you like to know?

Had he been in the military, like many airline pilots, and in Vietnam?

Yes.

Did he fly the hundred missions over the North?

"Yes. How do you know about that?"

The only pilot I knew who had been in Vietnam flew the required hundred missions to qualify to go home. After he did it, they changed the rules and he had to fly more exceedingly dangerous missions. He became so upset about the rule change that he developed a heart murmur and lost a promised airline job. Instead, he went to medical school.

"I got mad, but not that mad," Bob said. "Other things make me madder."

Such as?

"The new rules." He was holding back.

Security issues? the Acorn guest asked.

That's only part of it, he said. "It's guns. Everyone's allowed to carry guns when they come on my airplane except me. I am not allowed to carry a gun. In the old days we were like ship captains. Many of us carried a gun just in case something came up." Everyone stopped eating now to listen.

"My gun's locked up—well, that's great. If someone tries to hijack my plane, what am I supposed to say? 'Excuse me while I go unlock my gun'? Why even have a gun on the plane if it isn't available?"

"So who can bring a gun on a plane?" Acorn, who had been about to leave for her brunch, asked, sitting back down.

"Who? I'll tell you who." She had asked the right question and he was warming up.

"Marshals can bring guns on my plane. So can the FBI. So can the Secret Service, the Forest Service, and postal inspectors. Any of them can walk onto my airplane carrying a loaded .357 magnum and they aren't even trained how to shoot it in flight. I'm the only one who's trained to shoot a gun on an airplane but, remember, my gun's locked up."

Bob pushed back his chair, standing up. "Worse than that, someone legally carrying a gun on my airplane may not know that someone else legally carrying a gun is on board."

"I work for the federal government," Acorn said, "and I doubt they wouldn't know."

"So, what if one of them decides to get something out of a travel bag?" Bob leaned over to demonstrate. "As this person reaches down for his bag, which is under the seat in front of him, he leans way over, his jacket falls open and now anyone can see his gun!" Bob patted his pocket where the gun might be.

"What if someone else on the plane who sees this has a gun, too? Then I could have a gunfight on my hands and, don't forget, my gun is locked up."

Soon everyone was discussing planes, safety, whether we're a country that travels too much, the effects on family life, and so on. Eventually I remembered my duties and excused myself while the guests continued the conversation. It was time to get their bills ready. I had almost forgotten that these people were supposed to pay me.

Coyote Dreams

SUSIE PHONED EVERY DAY UNTIL HUGO CAME HOME and then she and Scott walked over with her homemade rolls and he carried lettuces from his garden so perfectly formed they looked like a bouquet of russet-edged green roses. Hugo seemed to gather strength from telling them about his scrape, although as soon as they left he lay down exhausted, and slept the rest of the day.

There were no bookings for the next weeks, so I set up office work on the dining room table while Hugo watched TV and napped. He woke up from these naps confused and I had to remind him where we were and why. He had trouble keeping track of time and became convinced that I changed all the clocks when he wasn't looking. He couldn't take his pills, the eleven pills a day that would save his life, our life together, and our dreams.

"Look at your watch," I suggested when it was time to take the pills. I set the bottles on a tray with a glass of water. He looked at the bottles, but didn't open them. I sat down beside him, opened each bottle, checked the dosage and handed him the pills one by one. We got through three before he needed more water. He swallowed slowly. I avoided looking at my watch.

The next time I went out I picked up two plastic pill cases at the drugstore, each with seven compartments clearly marked M T W T F S S. Problem solved.

"I'm not using those things," Hugo said the minute he saw them. "They're for old people."

"Yes, you are."

"No, I'm not."

"Do you want to die?"

He answered by clicking on the TV.

Even with the pillboxes, which I refilled every Sunday night, I watched over him taking the medicines. Too much blood thinner and he would bleed to death, too little and he might form more blood clots and have another stroke. The scariest of these high-powered medicines was the one that regulates heart rhythm. Too much of that one and his heart would stop, too little and he would have more arrhythmia, which could also trigger another stroke.

My own heart started fluttering, an unnerving sensation like a tiny bird trying to escape from inside my chest. Hugo sensed the toll his bad luck was taking and started trying to refill the pill cases himself. Pills spilled on the desk and floor, rolling under dusty furniture, and as I crawled around on my hands and knees trying to find them all so the cat wouldn't eat them, I tried hard not to cry. This phase seemed to go on forever and to extend forever back in time. There had never been anything but this. We were frozen in one awful moment.

One morning I sat down impatiently when it was time for him to take the medicine, and forced my eyes away from the clock.

"You can relax now," Hugo said. "I can take the pills myself." I watched him closely. He got it half-right. When I pointed out the mistake, the second box of pills unopened, his pride was hurt and he tossed the box in the air.

After that I waited until he was in bed for the night to check if the right boxes were empty. Two months later, when he called up and ordered his own refills from the pharmacy, I checked every other day. I still didn't trust the recovery. Whenever he went out, even to the garage, I insisted he take along his cell phone. When he tried to nap, I woke him up every fifteen minutes to see if he was all right. The shadow of his almost-death filtered into every corner of my mind. Life, I dimly perceived, will never be the same. Toughen up, I tried lecturing myself. Kiss life before the undertoad good-bye.

He had trouble separating dreams from reality and woke up shouting that the house was collapsing on Buck as he tried to jack it up. He dreamed that a hawk got Annabelle, our little black-and-white cat. Fully grown, she was the size of a large kitten and Hugo worried about her more than anything else. At least he's alive, I reminded myself, struggling to keep calm as I tried to think how I could juggle my day job and the bed-and-breakfast and look after Hugo. Because the doctors said he would recover completely, I went ahead and booked reservations, including a wedding party a year off, and sent out confirmations. Closing down the business, an obvious solution, could be bad for his psyche and his health. Most evenings Hugo sat down at the table where I worked and watched. He looked at the reservation book and the unopened bills and rearranged the envelopes. Weak and tired, he was alternately euphoric about being alive and depressed.

"Do you know what warfarin is?" he asked me almost daily, referring to the blood-thinning medicine. "It's rat poison. I'm a fifty-two-year-old white male being kept alive on rat poison."

As time passed, he said it more lightly and gradually I realized he meant it as humor. I laughed. At that he tried it out on the kids when they called. "I gather he's feeling better," Ethan observed with relief in his voice.

A few weeks after that I went back to my day job. Returning home from the office, I discovered that Hugo had booked a room and noted it in the reservation book, albeit in barely legible writing. His bills, now opened, were organized by due date and he even paid a few. Casually looking over his shoulder at his checkbook, I saw that he had forgotten to record the checks, so I opened the envelopes, he recorded the amounts, and we taped the envelopes closed. His handwriting slanted up across the checkbook page far outside the lines, but it marked a change.

If he could do even a little, I prayed I could hold everything together until some part-time help turned up. The children were all too far away to come more than a couple of weekends a year. Linda and Rick were too busy professionally to be counted on for more than that, and the same was true of close friends who volunteered. Although friends said it sounded like fun and wanted to experience running a bed-and-breakfast, it was unrealistic to think there would be any steady help and I had no way to put them up. The fledgling business could not support regular inn stays or even an inexpensive motel.

I longed for my mother, who at one time could have run the place all by herself. At ninety-two she was starting to feel her age and did not think she could travel. By phone she kept saying she only wished to be five years younger.

At least there wasn't a lot of time to worry because there was always something that needed doing. If the bed-and-breakfast didn't require attention, then Hugo did. He dreamed he heard coyotes yipping in the cornfield, then he started saying he heard coyotes for real. I thought it was his medications—until I started hearing them too.

One rainy dusk, a Saturday, he was watching TV while I made dinner. From the kitchen, I heard screams. It wasn't the TV. I went to the kitchen door. Unearthly screaming came from somewhere in the yard. In the deep shadows I made out Annabelle cornered between the magnolia and the brick path by a much larger cat or maybe a small collie. I ran outside, yelling and flailing my arms to chase it off. As it turned, I saw the distinctive, large straight-up ears, elongated muzzle, and bushy tail carried straight down of a coyote.

It gave me a long, cool stare before walking off along the formal path leading to the front of the house. Annabelle dashed for the kitchen door. That night, and every night after that, she refused to sleep downstairs and stayed outside our bedroom door where Hugo set a basket for her. I thought they were both overreacting until a few days later when I came downstairs in the morning to make coffee, found a rip in the screen door and long, tawny hairs caught in the jagged edge of the screen.

No one mentions coyotes unless you ask. "Ah, yes," Scott said when Hugo asked if it could really be a coyote I saw. "There are coyotes and red foxes around, too, but the coyotes are chasing the foxes away." It seems that coyotes expanded east of the Mississippi in the early twentieth century, though they did not arrive in Maryland until the 1970s. Based on their rate of increase in neighboring states like Virginia, coyotes are expected to increase here at a comparable rate of close to 30 percent a year.

Top-order predators, coyotes are secretive, wary, clever, and fast, and they are highly adaptable, especially in their food habits. They eat seasonally abundant plants, insects, mice, squirrels, birds, rabbits, deer, and livestock and have acquired a special taste for domestic cat.

Kitchen, Garden, Field

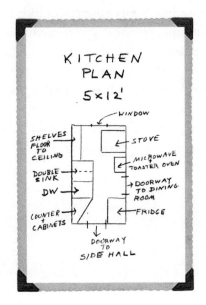

KITCHEN
PLAN
5×12'

WINDOW

SHELVES
FLOOR
TO
CEILING

STOVE

MICROWAVE
+
TOASTER OVEN

DOUBLE
SINK

DOORWAY
TO DINING
ROOM

DW

COUNTER
+
CABINETS

FRIDGE

DOORWAY
TO
SIDE HALL

AT FIRST I KEPT THE KITCHEN EXACTLY AS HUGO
had it. Over time I began reorganizing his domain, out of
necessity, moving basic equipment down to the lower shelves
where I could reach it without a stepladder and clearing the
countertops. I stacked cartons full of sauciers, mixing bowls,
ladles, immersion blenders, and three extra cast-iron pans, all
completely unnecessary in my view, and dragged them to the

back of the laundry room. A second electric mixer, two waffle irons, and a mandoline big enough for a cruise ship kitchen went under the desk.

He noticed but didn't say anything, except to bring out a favorite spatula and ask if we could make room for it. I didn't see why we needed four spatulas, but agreed. Normally, when Hugo was cooking, I entered the kitchen at my peril. Now I missed the aura created by his autocratic chef self, even if the kitchen was more orderly. When he was in charge, the food was better.

Returning from a porch visit with Susie in the middle of the summer, I walked into the kitchen and stopped short. The boxes of extra cookware I had stashed away blocked my path. Open cookbooks, flour, sugar, mixing bowls, cream, spices, and broken eggshells covered the counter, along with a cutting board full of chopped onions and red and green peppers, which spilled onto the floor. From the oven drifted the fragrance of cheese melding with eggs and herbs—chives, dill, maybe a little rosemary too.

Hugo, in a fresh shirt, his hair neatly brushed back, wore a new intent expression on his face. Smoothly he swung the oven door open, as I watched from the other side of the cartons, and spooned out a bit of breakfast pudding, blew on it, and raised the spoon up to my mouth.

Before the bed-and-breakfast opened, we'd questioned friends, family, the electrician, the painter, colleagues of mine at the museum, and other guests and hosts whenever we stayed at a bed-and-breakfast about what they liked to eat when they visited an inn. They all gave remarkably similar answers.

Strawberries, almost everyone said, and homemade bread or muffins, also a "baked egg thing." Strawberries were plentiful and grown locally. The baking was well in hand. But the "egg thing" was cause for concern. The director of the Talbot county tourism office, Debbi Dodson, remembered a bed-and-breakfast where all they served was "plain old scrambled eggs." Clearly this entrée staple, even if our eggs were cooked with fresh herbs, would have to go.

Hugo now considered fritattas, stratas, and variations on French toast—all delicious, but they didn't seem truly at home on the Eastern Shore. We started investigating traditional local favorites to celebrate the Chesapeake. Reading from a collection of historic recipes at the library, I learned that savory "puddings" were brought here by early English settlers and the dish caught on. It wasn't on any restaurant menus as far as I could tell, so I asked around. No one seemed to know about it until I happened on Kim, a physical therapy assistant and fourth-generation Eastern Shore resident. When I described what I meant by the pudding—bread soaked in egg and milk, layered with cheddar and sausage or ham, and baked, she said, "Whatever you call it, we always have that for Christmas. I love it."

Lucy and Amanda were less enthusiastic. Maybe, Lucy said. "You'll ruin the business if you give that to guests," Amanda advised. "It sounds gross." After they tasted it, they changed their minds and this Eastern Shore Pudding, served with local asparagus and potatoes crusted with Bay Spice, came to be a favorite with guests.

Looking around some more, we discovered that the farmers market, set up under shady trees overlooking St. Michaels harbor from spring to fall, offers a gorgeous selection of fresh cheeses, figs, red and green tomatoes, squash blossoms, berries, peaches, pears, sweet corn, and apples—all grown or made nearby—as well as country ham, a long-time local tradition. The first owner of the Pasadena Inn in Royal Oak once slaughtered a seven-hundred-pound hog and people reminisced that you could smell it for days smoking over apple wood. There are still folks around who will smoke a quarter-ham for you, perhaps in exchange for a second ham. A mixture of apple, cherry, and sassafras wood is considered about as good as it gets.

A creamy, aged cheddar with a delicate white rind at the market caught my attention. Sometimes it was available, other times not. Eventually I tracked down the cheese-maker on her family dairy farm in nearby Easton. At Chapel's Country Creamery, owned by Eric and Holly Foster, I saw Holsteins and Jerseys grazing on clover and rye. "The grass and the sun," Holly said, "that's what makes good milk and good cheese." In addition to the cheddar, cave-aged for a year, she had a soft, young cheese with an earthy, nutty flavor that was luscious, and I came home with both.

Then in the fall Hugo happened on a spindly persimmon tree behind an abandoned barn and gathered a basketful of the plump orange globes, bringing thoughts of persimmon bread and sweet persimmon pudding. Being native American foods, I tried my hand at these.

After the first frost, I walked down the driveway one day and found dark brown husks the size of golf balls scattered all over the road. I looked up and saw the tree from which they had fallen, its branches laden with more. On intuition I got a hammer and cracked one open. The unmistakable piquancy of black walnut took me back to my grandmother's kitchen, to black walnut cookies and cake. I remembered an old-fashioned milk cake baked in a cast-iron pan that would be perfect for these succulent nuts, so prized by former generations and forgotten by ours, probably because of how hard it is to pry them out of their shells. Our menus started coming together just by looking around, though sometimes it took an expert eye to tell us what exactly we were looking at. That winter, Roland stopped by and pointed out to Hugo that right at his feet bloomed lovely mounds of winter cress. "My sister really likes cress," he said. "She'll pick it where she can." We offered him some and brought more in the house to taste. Lacy, tender, crisp, and slightly bitter, these greens would complement almost any breakfast entrée.

Hugo conjectured that the guests would not be interested in "health foods" when on vacation and he was correct. Once in five years now has a guest asked for the "Health Breakfast" I offer of yogurt, honey, cinnamon, and fruit, along with whole-grain toast. Another quirk that took getting used to was the guests' appetite for croissants. I didn't see any reason to make or serve this French specialty on the Eastern Shore and only resorted to frozen supermarket croissants one Sunday when we ran short of homemade sticky buns for guests with big appetites. I warmed the croissants, dusted them with powdered sugar, and set them out. When it came time to clear the tables, it was a surprise to see that some poached pear remained on plates and a few bites of ham, but the croissant plate—licked clean.

For research purposes, I tried offering croissants again. The same thing happened. Even when guests requested just coffee and toast, I put out croissants. They might leave the toast, but never yet any croissants. At brunch, guests have even left some of Hugo's award-winning praline pumpkin pie, which took first prize one year in the St. Michaels contest, in favor of croissant. I finally tasted one to see what I was missing, but this confection, made entirely by robots and loaded with trans fats, was as gluey as I remembered.

No sooner were the centerpieces of the new breakfast menus set for the start of our second season, with one hot entrée offered each morning, than the health department arrived for a kitchen inspection. This was a new regulation in our state; some regions do not require inspection.

"Let's say you serve a breakfast-type pudding," the inspector said, walking briskly into the kitchen. "Would you set it up the night before, for example, mixing together the bread and eggs?" I caught Hugo's eye. Do these walls have ears or what?!

Hugo was ready. Drawing on his cooking school and obligatory sanitation training, he answered with confidence. "Never."

"Why not?" the inspector persisted.

Hugo described how raw egg, if it contained bacteria, would contaminate the bread if the refrigeration didn't hold steady below forty degrees and if the cooking heat was not high enough for long enough to kill bacterial growth.

The Royal Oak House kitchen passed inspection, as I expected, just as enthusiastic reviews of Hugo's breakfasts started rolling in. When return guests called to book, they'd often request the very same breakfast as before.

Hugo seemed a little better every day. We argued almost not at all and I dared to hope we were climbing back on track.

In some places it might be a big house or a big job that lets you "in," but around here trucks of a certain size are important and most men have two, a good truck along with an everyday work truck. Early on, Hugo had traded his sport-utility vehicle for a pickup, claiming he had a lot of construction materials and trash to haul around. Guns were also way up there in importance, and ever since the sheriff's gunfire welcomed us to town, Hugo had planned to look for his gun, untouched since military school days.

With one thing and another, he didn't get around to it until a lull after the start of the second season. He found his rifle, cleaned it, and had it checked out at the local gun shop ("Fire away, it's fine"). He bought some shells, and when there were no guests he practiced target shooting in the backyard. At his urging I practiced, too, just enough to know how to load, aim, fire, and not get hurt. The most shocking thing about it was how easy it was. The rifle looked and felt like a toy.

I wanted Hugo to get rid of the shells and put the gun away. Isn't there a statistic about how many people shoot family members by mistake? What if I came home late one night and he woke up thinking I was an intruder? He chose to ignore my advice. Luckily.

Digging a bed for zinnias under the bay windows, I was sitting on the grass with my back up against the house. The grass shifted as if riffled by a breeze and a long shadow crossed in front of me. It was large and weaving through the grass right in front of the bed I was digging.

As Simple As
It Seems

IT WAS ALMOST FIVE FEET LONG. I SCANNED MY MEMORY of snakes. It wasn't a copperhead, but I couldn't remember what a water moccasin looked like, just that they are the most aggressive, venomous snake on the Eastern Shore. Called *trapjaws*, they have a nasty habit of holding on when they bite. Their nonpoisonous water snake companions are less stout but without the two side by side, how could I say if this one was more or less stout? One water snake has round eyes, the moccasin has vertically elliptical cat's eyes. I was too afraid to look this snake in the eye. It was probably afraid of me, too. The difference was it had the entire yard and I couldn't move.

Hugo, who happened to be repainting the porch floor, somehow noticed, went inside, got the gun from the closet and shells from a drawer in another room, came around to the front of the house, down the steps, up alongside me, and aimed.

He missed and the snake took off.

190

Ten days later the snake came back and hung around the back porch. This time Hugo did not miss. I felt a rush of gratitude, followed by fear. What would have happened if the fates were unkind and Hugo had not been out and around or not around at all? It was impossible to forget the recent past—it reared up at the slightest opportunity—and it seemed clear to me now that the fates had flirted with taking Hugo away, then capriciously, or who knows why, decided not to.

When Roland next came by—Roland, who possesses more practical knowledge of the area's natural history than anyone else we know—Hugo mentioned shooting the snake.

"Those big poisonous snakes can be annoying and they will hang around a place. You did the right thing, Hugo. You did the right thing." Roland switched off his truck engine, opened the door, and climbed down.

Hugo had suddenly gained stature because, as Roland went on to say, snakes are hard to hit. Sean, who worked at The Oaks, saw us gathered at the roadside and came over. Roland always brought interesting news and if anything was up in Royal Oak, he probably knew it. He is also the person the weekend people call when a raccoon, snake, or fox gets in their barn, chimney, or house.

Sean said snakes like to hang from the branches of the huge white oaks down by the inn's dock, but the guests did not like this at all. It was Sean's job to get rid of them. "If it's high up in a tree, I'll shoot it. But if it's just lying on the ground, I'll pick it up by the tail and heave it as far as I can in the field."

I realized a macho contest was underway and got busy deadheading the roses.

"If it bites," Sean was saying, "don't go and yank its head off you because the teeth are weak. They'll break off and stay in your skin and you'll get a nasty infection. You have to wait till the snake decides to let go."

Roland: "Shovel's the best way, as far as I'm concerned, Hugo. If it's on the ground, smack it on the head. Now if a snake makes my brother mad, I'll tell you what he does, especially if it's poisonous. He'll take it in his two hands and just rip it apart, like you snap a belt."

The subtext of Sean and Roland's advice could not have been clearer. You did pretty good for a come-here, but you've still got a few things to learn.

It went like that whenever Hugo or I thought we were there, settled, getting comfortable, had learned what we needed to know to move on. It reached a point that I started wondering ahead of time what lessons the next day or hour, guests or neighbors would bring. Every time I guessed wrong.

"You aren't Democrats, are you?" The question was inescapable, whether it came over the fence, at a party, picnic, or happy hour gathering, though it wasn't always put so directly. The answer was obvious in the newspapers you read and mentioned. Around election time it was more than obvious in the signs you posted in your front yard, or not, and the bumper stickers you displayed on your truck, or not. Only once did the question come straight at me and there wasn't even time to say *independent* before this neighbor went on to add, "Because we can't stand for anyone to be against our boys, our troops, like the Democrats are."

Safe topics of conversation were gardening, a new restaurant because it was such a novelty that everyone checked it out right away, and encounters with wildlife.

An encounter with wildlife is probably the highest-status topic and I've gathered that if you haven't had any lately it's okay to make one up. At a girls-only party I was pleased to be invited to, I met a sweet-faced older woman who concocts the best chicken salad with green grapes I've ever tasted. When I sat down to ask her for details of the recipe, I noticed her foot in a cast. What happened? She was out shooting a raccoon that was trying to get at the barn swallows' nest, she explained, when the rifle kicked back so hard she tripped and broke her ankle. But she got the raccoon.

"She wasn't out shooting any raccoon," her daughter told me the next day. "She broke her ankle at a yard sale."

Development, of course, is not a safe subject. The spread of big box stores over vast tracts of farmland is widely welcomed because it brings jobs, lower prices, and more convenient shopping. Even the old standby, the weather, is not a safe subject because of its inevitable, inconvenient connection to climate and politics. Hugo learned this around the neighborhood and he had to learn it over again from the guests.

Looking out the window on a mid-December day at the flowering quince in our front yard, a guest asked what it was. Hugo told him and then lapsed, remarking that the quince usually blooms in early April. "But there's no such thing as global warming, is there?"

The guest bristled. "There certainly is not. What there is is an effort to discredit our hardworking leadership in Washington."

Exactly, Hugo answered, trying to retain a shred of poise, along with his self-respect.

Back in the kitchen, he scowled. Slam-dunked again.

At that time it was unimaginable that a perceptible shift in attitude would ever take place. It started when Vice-President Dick Cheney, a part-time resident a few miles away, accidentally shot a fellow quail hunter in Texas. At the gun store Hugo fell into discussion. Everyone agreed it was unfortunate, but the man who sold Hugo shells expressed the prevailing sentiment most succinctly. "Thanks to heaven the vice-president didn't shoot that lawyer in the face anywhere around here! He would have screwed our safety record."

A newspaper editorial calculated how long it would take to repair damage to the statistics if the vice-president had shot someone in Talbot County. In any event, much care is taken during hunting season and almost everyone who walks, jogs, or bicycles wears blaze orange. One neighbor sports a penitentiary-orange jumpsuit and a welder's mask when he ventures out because not even a local knows when birdshot will come flying out of the woods.

A bigger shift in acceptable subject matter occurred as the Iraq war worsened. The jabs at Democrats and suspected Democrats stopped—they just stopped cold—as if this had never been a major sport, and politics altogether faded to an almost nonexistent topic. I wasn't sure about this until the heating and air-conditioning repairman came by to check the furnace.

As he wrote out the invoice, he said he guessed we wouldn't be needing the furnace half as much as the air-conditioning this year. It was a really good thing we had finally put it in. "The industry journals we get, they all say it—and I don't know what side you're on politically, but I can tell you—this thermal warming thing they talk about, it's happening, it's here."

Even before all that, dodging political discussions was easier than avoiding hidden conversational land mines, of which there seem to be an unlimited number.

Like the pigs.

Driving out to a farmstand on St. Michaels Road, I passed a new fenced enclosure of animals and slowed down for a better look. Definitely pigs. Someone had tried to start a garden center on the site, but owing to regulations or politics, the garden center was not allowed. The nursery stock already dug into the ground was dying. The newly arrived pigs, I saw, were large and robust.

A few weeks later when I drove by again, I was startled to see a rusty old station wagon parked inside the pigpen, tires flat, doors open. Spray-painted on the windows in fluorescent pink and green was "OINK-OINK." Within days the pigs, as could only be expected of pigs, issued their own scatological statement. More weeks later, pigs, car, and fencing vanished, as if they had never been.

Meanwhile, a couple of miles closer to town a new business opened up with a field full of too many hundreds of recreational vehicles, boats, and trailers to count. It reminded me of what Eugene McCarthy, who once lived along the Chesapeake watershed, observed: "Nothing in the country is ever quite as simple as it seems."

When I ventured to ask a knowledgeable local about the curious appearance and disappearance of the pigs, it was my turn to be slam-dunked. "Those animals belong to a very nice family. The family owns a lot of land around here, always have."

Sticking to wildlife sightings is a safer bet and it's one of the best surprises of our new life. "I saw a Monarch," someone will greet you. "Just one, but they're on the way." A shopper at the market says, "I hear quail in the woods again. They were gone so long, it's wonderful to have them back." Scott Kilmon reports, "The barn swallows are here" and "Got the first striper yesterday." A boat captain announces, "The ospreys are back in their nest on channel marker nine."

I've started to join in. "For the first time I saw a ruby-throated hummingbird," I say at the farmers market. "It was feeding on my trumpet vines and when it flew away I saw gold dust, pollen, on its beak and throat." The farmer who sells sweet corn was impressed, but don't try to one-up anyone with your sightings.

"Do you know what my cat did yesterday?" she answered. "She brought a baby rabbit in the house and I found them napping side by side."

The cat wanted a pet? I asked. "Oh, no. The cat has done this before and I always set the baby rabbit free before the cat can carry out her evil plan."

Guests and Geese

THERE ARE SO MANY GOOD GUESTS THAT WHEN A BAD
one turns up, it always comes as a surprise. It was June, I
remember, because the scent of honeysuckle mingled with the
deep aroma of cigar smoke as we rounded the driveway after
a late-night walk. Laughter echoed from the front porch and I
saw the orange glow of sparks as a smoker tapped away ashes.
The voice of Ella Fitzgerald drifted from the open front door
of our house.

Men in tuxes and women in cocktail dresses sat on the porch. A pleasing sight except for the sparks and the door open to mosquitoes, wasps, snakes, foxes, coyotes, and who knew what else. Maybe we should stay up, I suggested to Hugo as we slipped discreetly in the side door, to monitor the party.

"Not necessary." They seemed exceptionally polite and courteous when they requested an ice bucket earlier, he reported, and they'd asked permission to smoke on the porch.

It was too late to bake the almighty muffins anyway, so I set the alarm and sank into bed. Hugo watched the late news on TV and followed me upstairs.

All seemed well. In the morning the muffins got baked on time. The polite guests ate, paid, and left. The charges went through on their credit cards.

The next day as incoming guests drove up, Hugo asked what I had done with the CDs in the parlor. He wanted to put on some music.

Nothing, I told him.

"Well, they aren't here. You must have put them away."

"Nope."

"I'm looking for jazz—you know, Mulligan, Miles, Ella, Parker, Sarah Vaughan, any of the good jazz stuff."

He settled for a new-age CD that we occasionally used as background. After checking the guests in, we hunted around, opening and closing drawers all over the house. Every jazz recording was gone.

"Damn, I hate guests!" Hugo said.

"You left too many CDs lying around," I pointed out. These particular guests were visiting from a part of the world where a jazz collection like that would be difficult if not impossible to assemble. I felt betrayed at the loss, but more embarrassed by our own inexperience.

I quickly set it aside as just another lesson learned. But Hugo brought it up for weeks, getting upset again at each retelling. He seemed less resilient than the old Hugo, who would have been joking about it by now.

A couple sat at a table by the window in the dining room. I said good morning and set down their breakfasts. No response. As I started moving away to the next table, the woman spoke up. "Is there a drugstore around here?"

That explained it. She wasn't feeling well. I gave directions and noticed that she seemed to have a shiner, probably painful.

She went upstairs and he briefly went out. Then they stayed in their room all day. An innkeeper has to notice such things to avoid disturbing guests when they want privacy.

Late in the afternoon I passed them in the hall as they were on their way out, all dressed up. He in jacket and tie, she in a smart black dress. I saw bruises up and down one arm. The shiner was mostly concealed under makeup.

Worrisome. I considered the possibilities of physical abuse, drugs, or that it was just a normal course of events. My body looked something like that while we were doing construction.

The next morning when neither of these guests appeared for breakfast, I told Hugo my fears. Complete silence came from the direction of their room. The woman could be dead from a drug overdose or a blow. At 10:30 I cleared away their untouched breakfasts. A few minutes after 11:00, checkout time, we discussed what to do. Knock on their door or run the vacuum cleaner in the hall outside their door? Hugo knocked and I started up the vacuum.

A muffled man's voice from the other side of the door said they were getting ready to leave and needed more time. At noon they walked down the driveway to their car.

The room was an ugly sight. Empty beer bottles filled with cigarette butts and, thoughtfully, water lined the windowsills. The room would have to be aired, all the linens, pillows, coverlet, and curtains washed before we could book it again. The "No Smoking" sign was upside down in the dresser drawer. I found two more drawers filled with neatly folded women's clothing. Apricot and green T-shirts, shorts, brightly embroidered skirts, belts, hats, a shawl. Clothes for a happy time.

Grateful that there weren't any dead bodies, I packed the clothing in a box and stored it on a shelf in the laundry room. A violent incident could seriously damage the reputation of our fledgling business. In a small town people talk, of course, and they remember.

Everyone remembers and still talks about a woman who plotted to poison her husband at a murder-mystery weekend held by a local golf resort. Friends thought she was joking until the sheriff opened an investigation into his death. The judge, clearly shocked, described it as a Hamlet-like play within a play and she was sentenced to thirty years in prison.

The resort survived this, and St. Michaels holds securely to its reputation as a charming, quaint, very nice town—the town with no traffic light, the town that fooled the British. Maybe we could survive an awful event, too, but I was left with a heavy heart, wondering about my responsibility to guests. Where does being nosy end and caring concern begin?

Then came the guests who wished to observe their religious holiday. They would relax, stay in, talk, and eat with their friends. For twenty-four hours the world would be closed out. I envied the beauty and serenity of this, and said so.

Never did I suspect that their rituals involved filling my cracked, antique washbowl, a gift from an old friend, with water and floating sticky brown candles in it. Water and wax leaked out and the wax got all over the white bath towels. I tried heat, stain remover, and bleach before cutting the towels into pure cotton cleaning rags. Neither did I guess that these guests would stock in enough food to feed a village. Straightening their rooms after the first night, I found platters mounded high with fried chicken, salads, breads, and cake. There were fruits, candies, bottles of wine, juice, and soda everywhere. It was impossible to know what to do, so I just left everything.

When these guests departed, Hugo went in the parlor to check on things and ran into big black plastic trash bags, loaded with empty bottles and leftover food, that were leaking onto the rose Bordeaux rug. I wondered about a holiday that allowed them to waste so much and wondered if they stored garbage bags in the middle of their own living rooms.

At times like this it was tempting to blame everything on Hugo. The first time I allowed myself a flash of anger since his illness was over these guests. You, I pointed out, are the one who decided to open our home to *complete strangers.* What did you expect!?

Yes, he did that, but I learned something, too, and it wasn't flattering. I've learned that it takes true generosity of spirit to run a bed-and-breakfast right. You can run one any which way, but to do it right takes something more. Yes, I like helping an elderly guest up the stairs, carrying his glass of sherry so he can hold onto my arm with one hand and the banister with the other. I like welcoming guests and seeing that they are comfortable and well cared for. I enjoy their smiles, their thank-yous for a wonderful, restful time. But the religious celebrants taught me that I might come up short in the generosity department. I might come up short the next time guests act up.

I've learned that the excitement and discoveries this life offers are countered by the delusions and mysteries it strips away. In the end, like so many endeavors, it's about yourself. Do you have the heart to do it right?

This is not to suggest that we are model innkeepers—far from it. The worst faux pas so far? Well, Hugo was exasperated when guests backed their car into an iron flowerpot four feet high, knocking it over and cracking bricks on the walkway. A crash from the driveway drew his attention as we were clearing the breakfast tables. From the dining room window he saw the driver get out of his car to reposition the pot.

"Dumbasses!" Hugo fumed, violating Innkeeper Rule Two, which is second only to Rule One about *not* contacting guests when they leave valuables behind. Rule Two is to *never* talk about guests before they have checked out and left the county. You might see them go out with golf clubs, but you might not see them come back in. You might see their car drive off to a dinner reservation you yourself booked for them, but both guests might not be in the car.

"Be quiet!" I hissed. "The guests might hear you."

You worry too much, Hugo said. He had seen all the other guests all go out half an hour before. I glanced around the corner into the parlor and there of course sat one of the guests, looking up from his newspaper.

Hugo was mortified and visibly subdued for weeks after that—and I would have lectured him mercilessly on his gaffe, if this had happened before adversity shook my priorities into better order. But it was definitely this very experience that saved him from a terrible mistake when the worst of all visitors showed up.

A hotel will often "hold" rooms for events such as weddings, but a small inn can't because you might be left with no bookings at all. Even one no-show at a three-room inn means a big bite out of a slim income. Booking a room, we tell callers, requires a one-night paid deposit.

When a man asked to hold all our rooms for his wedding, Hugo explained the policy. He never sent in a deposit and many months later we booked the rooms for other guests. On the weekend in question, six young women carrying suitcases and garment bags arrived on our front porch, introducing themselves as the bridesmaids. I cringed. Hugo told them there were no reservations.

Less than five minutes after they left, a man in shorts, sweatshirt and ball cap on backward pounded on the door. It was the groom. Furiously chewing gum, he advanced toward Hugo, who again explained the policy and apologized.

The fist came up fast. Hugo closed his eyes and turned away. When he opened his eyes he was surprised that he was unharmed.

The groom evidently controlled himself at the last second and was walking away, but not before flinging open the gate so hard it snapped its antique hinges. At least he was gone. The gate could be fixed. One guest in almost a thousand.

"I wish I'd flattened him," Hugo said that night. He was more upset than I had seen him since a customer over fifteen years before shoplifted a book from his store. When we went to bed, I rested my head on his chest and felt his heart beating in a wildly irregular pattern. "Are you going to be all right?" I asked, probably for the hundredth time. He said his heartbeat was often like that, it was just a new fact of life, what all the eleven pills were for.

For my part, I started expecting trouble. Maybe a bed-and-breakfast is bad for him, maybe he'll die doing it, I worried. Alternately I tried to contain my fears, important if we hoped to beat the odds of burning out, which in this business run high. At times like this, I got in the habit of sitting down to reread notes left online or in the guest book. One of my favorites:

> Thank you for a respite from the "real" world.
> After all the real world is right here.

10.13.07
OUR SECOND VISIT, & LIKE THE FIRST, WONDERFULL'
RELAXING WITH EARLY NIGHTS & EARLY MORNINGS, FELINE
BENEDICTIONS CARE OF ANNABEL... EXACTLY WHAT WE
WANTED & NEEDED. WE'LL BE BACK (HOPEFULLY THAT ISN'T
TAKEN LIKE A THREAT)... WE NEED MORE BEAUTIFUL
EASTERN SHORE DAYS AND SUNSETS OVER THE CORNFIELD

Another favorite came from a friend of Hugo's and a for-mer bookstore employee, Evan Parker, whose business card read, "Surreal and Fantastic Art, commissions accepted."

Two state-of-the-art Harleys roared into the driveway. Now it's our turn, I expected, to host Hells Angels. I looked for Hugo but he and his truck were gone and I seemed to remember him saying something about steak, beer, and laundry soap.

Two couples were booked for the steamy, late August weekend. There was no telling if these were the guests or "drop-ins" hoping for a last-minute vacancy.

I watched from the office window as riders in black leather dismounted from each bike. When they removed their helmets I saw two men and two women. A small Hells Angel contingent at least.

As they headed up the path between the boxwoods, I tried to compose my expression. At worst they will trash the place. *If it can be fixed,* I heard my mother's and grandmother's inter-twined voices saying, *it isn't so bad.*

And if they torch the place, then like phoenixes we'll start over again. Starting over, I decided, has its charms. A new start generates amazing energy.

I went out alone to greet the guests. The first sign that I might have jumped to the wrong conclusion was the absence of piercings or tattoos. We shook hands as they introduced themselves. The women were laughing.

"We only do this a couple of times a year, fortunately," one said, rolling her eyes at the guys and straightening her pearl necklace. "Now that they have to sit at desks all day like grown-ups, they like to get out once in a while and pretend they're kids."

Never do I ask guests about their work, with the thought that if they want to discuss it they will, and if not, if they are seeking a rest from the "real world," so be it. That's often why they have chosen to come here in the first place, to a quiet countryside bed-and-breakfast.

The next morning Hugo went out as they were suiting up, getting ready to tour the area, and admired the glinting bikes. It came up that the guys supervised a new three-state security detail of motorcycle police. They offered to take us out for a spin. I had no intention of going, but Hugo looked tempted, even as he thanked them for the offer.

Someone wants to book a room but is asking if the place is haunted, Hugo said, covering the receiver with his hand. What do we tell her? The husband is afraid of ghosts.

Wanting the business, I suggested the obvious: no ghosts here.

They came, stayed. No complaints. That seemed to settle the ghost question until about a month later, when a newspaper reporter turned up, wanting to know about the history of the place and the ghosts.

There aren't any, we both said. She expressed disappointment, which taught me that some want ghosts with their bed-and-breakfast and some don't. It taught me again that you can't please everyone. To make up for the absence of ghosts, I told her that ghosts are a popular subject in our village—in the whole area for that matter—and almost everyone else does have stories. Writer Helen Chappell, who lives nearby, specializes in them. You'll even find a ghost story now and again on the front page of the *Star Democrat,* which invites you to contact the community editor if you suspect that your house is haunted.

Have you been hearing strange things at night? . . .
Whether your historic home is inhabited by a 19th-century
apparition, or your neighbor has been having ghostly
visitors, the *Star Democrat* wants to hear about it.
—October 20, 2005

A long-experienced innkeeper told us he gets the question, too, and he has learned to respond with, "Do you want there to be ghosts?"

Aside from the ghosts of Zia Lillia and Mrs. Jefferson, personal ghosts invented for my own amusement, the only ghosts whose presence I sense are of geese. At first I found the opening of goose season exciting, the sound of their melodious calls marking the change of seasons from summer to fall, winter to spring, the first crack of gunfire bringing anticipation of a warming supper.

The Eastern Shore lies squarely on the Atlantic Flyway and Canada geese pass through in enormous, sky-darkening clouds. In autumn the geese travel south with their young of the year and the family remains together through the winter. In spring the yearlings follow their parents back to the nesting territory where they were born. The fields where corn and other grains have been harvested provide plenty of sustenance for their journeys between Canada and as far away as Mexico.

A regal, white-cheeked, long-necked bird, the Canada goose, *Branta canadensis,* has adapted well to trimmed lawns and ponds; it also frequents city parks and golf courses. Where winters are mild, Canada geese may not migrate at all. When migrating they can reach extraordinary speed, up to sixty miles an hour, and may fly at high altitudes. A Royal Oak neighbor, Francine, reported seeing them from her airplane at sixteen thousand feet. At this altitude, she explained to me, the geese go into a trancelike state that allows them to survive the thin air as they cruise on wind currents with an occasional, efficient flap of wing. Because it is the most tiring job, they take turns leading their aerodynamic, V-shaped formations. On the ground one goose, or two, always serves as a sentinel for the others. Hawks and coyotes will try to pick off the younger, smaller geese.

Overhunting and habitat loss in the early twentieth century took a severe toll on their numbers. Now, as a result of protection programs, there are millions, and geese have become pests in some areas, contaminating swimming beaches and waterways.

Hunting geese and ducks for sustenance has been important to Eastern Shore life, going back to the native tribes who hunted with bow and arrow and fashioned decoys from reeds. Later, hunting for sport led to the establishment of lodges, clubs, and guide services. The latest twist on decoys, for $150 each, is a goose decoy that turns its head right and left, powered by rechargable lithium batteries. At the gun shop a clerk reported selling these decoys to just one customer last season. The man bought a dozen and set them up in his field. Almost immediately a goose landed—and departed—the first and last goose lured with a battery-operated decoy.

Still in all, the more I saw out our window the less happy I was. I liked knowing about a goose's powers of navigation, its strength, and cleverness. I liked knowing that a large number of geese flying together is called a flock while geese on the ground are a gaggle, and a small number of geese flying together is a creche. From the window I saw that when a goose is shot down, its mate will circle in the sky for long minutes over the place where the bird fell, giving off unforgettable, plaintive cries. It's a sight that cuts deep. I'll stop what I'm doing to go out into the field and stare up at a lone circling goose. On one of these occasions Hugo came out and stood beside me. "Don't worry," he said. "It won't happen to us."

"You know that?"

"Yes. Just like I knew that this new life would bring us closer."

"I didn't really think you had another woman. It was fear and insecurity talking," I said, rushing on to get out what was really on my mind. I regretted not contributing more to the project. I gave as much time and money as I could, but never once stopped to ask if it was enough. I told him about opening a letter addressed to him, months ago, and finding out that he had borrowed on margin to finish work on the house. It upset me more than I could say.

"Did that make you sick?"

"It wasn't your fault," he said quietly, putting an arm around me. "Let's go inside."

I count the weeks and it's always a relief when goose season ends, although I still hear their cries long after the last flocks leave.

More Light

HUGO WAS SO MUCH STRONGER, EXCEPT FOR DIZZINESS behind the wheel of the truck, that I managed to almost forget the shadow over us for weeks at a time. I still kept watch for signs of slipups or confusion on his part. Claiming forgetfulness, I slyly asked him the date or when the next guests were arriving. Usually he was right. As for his persistent clumsiness, this distressed him more than it did me.

When he jumped down from the back of the truck, tripped, and fell, he sprained an ankle, but mostly injured his pride. Regularly he knocked over dishes, dropped knives. I sort of liked the sounds, a comforting backdrop to his presence, and it didn't matter to the guests because I served breakfast. Whatever happened in the kitchen no one saw or heard.

The more insistent question was whether he would stabilize at this level, improve further, or lose ground. If worrying about it would have helped, I would have worried. The doctors were noncommittal so there was nothing to do, as far as I could see, but hope and be grateful for what was. My best friend is fragile, but I still have him, I reminded myself at the slightest twinge of impatience at his new ways.

Reservations flowed in steadily. Hugo eventually took over all the paperwork, with me looking over his shoulder. I breathed easier, and easier still after his dad called up to say he thought stress wasn't good for Hugo. More, he said Zia Lillia had left money and he wanted us to pay off the start-up costs for the bed-and-breakfast.

Deciding all was quite well enough for me to visit my mother, I went. New acquaintances invited Hugo to dinner while I was gone so he wouldn't have to eat alone. When he arrived, he knew right away that something was wrong.

As our second season wound down, it seemed like a good idea to put up more lights around the place. The village café had colored lights and at night, without any streetlights, it made finding the café much easier. Even with a lighted sign and lampposts at the entrance to our driveway, some guests had trouble with the turn at a sharp curve on the dark road. So we strung up tiny white lights along the fence, three strings at first, then five, then eleven. Instantly business picked up and we congratulated ourselves on this clever, almost free advertising.

A muscular guy in tan camo fatigues at the back of the porch half-stood when introductions were made, then sat down with his drink and watched Hugo.

Deciding the food table was the safest place to be, Hugo pulled up a chair and finished off most of the ribs, greens, and cornbread. The man's girlfriend sat down next to Hugo and asked him a friendly stream of questions about the bed-and-breakfast, what we serve for breakfast, where we came from, and so on. Flattering, but he had already decided to leave as soon as he decently could, edgy about her companion at the other end of the room watching him. When conversation fell quiet, he heard ice cubes being sucked up and dropped one at a time back into a glass.

Finally, she got to the point. Her boyfriend can't stand seeing anything wasted, she said, but what annoys him most is when people waste natural resources. When a neighbor kept on a lot of lights all night, he said he wanted to kill the guy. She was afraid he meant it and begged him not to go over there in the middle of the night to confront the electricity wasters.

Hugo left the party right after that and in the morning he took down some of the fence lights.

This is not to suggest that the local impulse to conserve is any less than exemplary. Conservation is practiced in many ways. The thrift shops, for instance, did thriving business among people from all stations in life long before a deep recession made it nationally popular. In a place where goods were often in short supply over the centuries and anything that wasn't produced from the land had to arrive by boat, people learned to save and reuse.

To a jaded outsider, the trait can seem eccentric. A woman's pink plastic-handled mirror dangling from bicycle handlebars by a string, for example. At the sound of an approaching car or truck, the bicyclist lifts the mirror so he can see the oncoming vehicle. If only more of the country practiced conserving to a fraction of this degree!

The incident set me to thinking about our place in the village. Most of the time we felt comfortable, almost like insiders. People greeted us, waved when they drove by the house, the mail truck driver honked whenever he saw us outside. Without asking my name, Miss Ebbie at the post office brought out our mail.

People shared gossip about who wasn't speaking to whom, and why. One man didn't like the way another was developing his land. Another didn't like the way someone else used his own property for storage, and so on. The details weren't important—it was being included that mattered.

Over drinks with Susie and Scott one night as disputes among the neighbors were being reviewed, I decided to ask the question that had been on my mind almost since we arrived in town. How long, if ever, until we're not come-heres?

Scott threw back his head and laughed, relishing the opening I unwittingly provided. "There was a lady who came here from Baltimore as a newborn, not more than a week old," he said slowly. "When she died—" He paused and still I didn't guess what was coming.

"A newborn when she came here," he repeated. "When she died, the newspaper obituary read, 'Baltimore Woman, 90, Dies in Royal Oak.'"

• • •

I began to sense a rhythm to the acceptance dance, or maybe I imagined one. As a curtain was raised, the next one stayed lowered for a good long while. Let's see how you do with this much access, seemed to be the idea.

Down at the farmers market it was much the same. After many shopping trips, a layer of formality fell away unexpectedly late one Saturday morning when most of the crowd was gone. I ventured to ask Linda Wilson, the organic vegetable vendor, if she ever had green tomatoes. Sure, she said. She was just waiting for them to ripen before setting them out. I bought them all.

Feeling more confident, I asked at the next stand about the tiny milk-white eggs in small plastic boxes lined with paper toweling. Quail, Charlene said.

How do you cook them? Boil or poach, she said, adding, "Some people on a special occasion will devil them." I looked again at the miniature eggs. Even a demitasse spoon would be too big for these yolks. There was something in her voice that made me try the joke about how life is too short to stuff a mushroom. Charlene looked startled, then broke into a wide smile. That day I went home with a box of the eggs and an invitation to visit her farm to see the quail.

Her most spectacular fall offering was huge, ugly, mottled brown-green pears, the most juicy essence of pearness I ever tasted. She said the tree was old in her grandfather's time and no one knew the variety. I always ate a pear on the spot, dripping juice across my shirt and up to my elbows, before heading off to the Pot Pie Farm stand for a dozen chicken eggs with their hazy brown, green, and blue shells, creations of the farm's Araucanas and Buff Orpingtons.

For guests I experimented with poaching the pears in water with a dash of honey to highlight their delicacy. Hugo, looking on, asked if I would mind if he added this and that to the pears the next time. "They're a little plain for guests."

"As a matter of fact I do mind." He seemed so well by now that I allowed myself the luxury of what had never seemed like a luxury before, giving him a hard time. I craved it, the squabbling that comes with being completely comfortable in your private world with your mate, a world where you understand and are understood and everyone will live forever. The difference now was that I only went partway. Another part of me stood back, enjoying this new sport, only half meaning it.

"Just how fancy does everything have to be? I'm not good enough to poach pears?" He backed off but I kept at him, saying he could do all the cooking by himself from now on. After more discussion we agreed that the kitchen was not all his, like before, but mostly his. We agreed that he was a Kitchen Nazi. Friends thought I was crazy: He cooked and I didn't have to be in the kitchen—what a joy! The problem was I liked cooking and disliked being second-guessed when I tried my hand at something more creative than making juice and coffee.

The next time he poached the pears in grape juice.

"You've ruined them," I announced just before he opened the door to the dining room and the waiting guests. "They're actually cloying."

The time after that, I poached the pears in water, added star anise and vanilla, and he added dashes of color and flavor with orange and lime zest to finish the plates. It became the favorite of all the first courses we offer, aside from the croissants.

It finally happened, of course, after we had given up hope—the day we stopped being come-heres. Naturally, it had everything to do with the arrival in our midst of new newcomers. Car break-ins were occurring at the time, a first as far as anyone could remember. People who had never locked car or house doors before started locking up at night. Hugo, Susie, Scott, and I, out for pizza with two new week-end neighbors from Manhattan, were concerned that house robberies might be next.

A few days before, Scott had told Hugo he moved his guns upstairs—just in case. Speaking clearly, so all of us could hear, Scott asked if Hugo had moved his guns upstairs yet. I saw immediately what he was up to and admired the subtle reference to the 1812 British attack on St. Michaels when townspeople, according to legend, moved lights up to the church belfry and high windows.

"Yep."

"Good," Scott nodded, as Kurt's eyes widened. "Shells, too?"

"Yep," Hugo said again.

"Guns? Upstairs? You have a gun?" Kurt looked at Hugo with incredulity, betrayal in his voice. He all but said, *I thought you were like us.*

"Glad to hear you took the advice." Scott was savoring the effect of the conversation on the newcomers. "Makes sense, doesn't it? I mean no reason to take chances."

Hugo nodded gravely. I managed to wait until we got home for a high five.

And The Creek
Don't Rise

THESE DAYS FRIENDS AND ACQUAINTANCES DRIVE OUT
from Washington or from one of the airports in spring or summer, sometimes calling ahead, sometimes not. They look over
the house and garden, and settle on the porch with a cool drink
before asking the question. So: How do you like retirement?

No one hears the answer, I think, because what we do
doesn't look exactly like work. Conversation proceeds. They
comment on the restful setting and propose activities like
bicycling, sailing or kayaking, doing the Maritime Museum,
and finishing up with dinner.

Lovely plans, Hugo and I have learned to respond. Have
fun and we'll meet you for dinner if it's not too late. It's awkward to point out that they are on vacation and we're not.
If pressed, one of us will start listing the day's tasks: reservations to confirm, phone requests to answer, shopping for
breakfast because our tiny kitchen has little storage space. If
it isn't the housekeeper's day to help and one or more rooms
has to be "turned," meaning guests are checking out and new
ones are arriving on their heels, then Hugo and I will do it. A

pillowcase might need touching up if the housekeeper forgot to iron in sharp creases. I insist on this because it's the only way a guest can be certain the pillowcase is absolutely fresh. Once, when I knew the incoming guest was a surgeon, I even ironed the top sheet. This alarmed Hugo.

"Nice of you," he said. "But probably not necessary." I knew a surgeon would notice, but Hugo clearly thought my obsessive tendency was out of control.

If visitors don't get the picture yet, I'll continue with the list: yard trim to rake, garden benches to wash, walkways and steps to sweep, fresh flowers to cut, and maybe less routine matters, like ordering business cards or checking the minutes of the business association meeting to see if any new regulations are being planned for bed-and-breakfasts. Inspecting bed-and-breakfast kitchens, a recent rule, was clearly good for the industry. We were less sure about the one requiring bed-and-breakfasts that offer complimentary sherry to registered guests to serve it to anyone who walks in off the street and asks for it. We chose not to share news of that particular regulation around the neighborhood except with trusted friends.

The usual is to start work early so breakfast prep can be finished before going out for dinner with friends. Hugo has tried it the other way, starting kitchen work after a leisurely evening out, but by then guests in the bedroom above the kitchen are usually back from their evening and trying to sleep. He can't turn on the mixer, sauté peppers and onions, which means switching on a noisy vent fan, or let pans clank without disturbing the guests.

Eventually, if not when friends arrive then by the next day, the idea may dawn on them that we have not "retired."

It is redefinition or dreamchasing, maybe some of both. It is definitely work.

As for those who don't get it, I've decided that if they want to think of us as "retired," so be it. I choose to consider it a compliment, the sign of a job done well enough that it seems effortless.

Back at the museum I found myself explaining to the summer interns that we didn't spend all day in the galleries looking at art and that I closed the express mail office more nights a year than I wanted to count. In this regard little has changed. I find myself explaining that we don't sit on the porch all day sipping mint juleps. What I don't say, because our visitors are in an up, light mood: When you've come this close to losing everything, it's all good and, exactly as my sister had foreseen, it's all easy.

The bed-and-breakfast community proved welcoming locally and beyond. After several seasons I was surprised one afternoon by a phone call from the state bed-and-breakfast association asking if Hugo would be willing to inspect a bed-and-breakfast that was applying for membership. Hugo said he didn't feel qualified to pass judgment on others. I reminded him that we had passed the state's 135-point inspection with high marks. The purpose of this inspection is to ensure the public of basic standards of safety, comfort, and convenience. Criteria include general cleanliness, appropriate amenities for guests like good reading lights, adequate exterior lighting, general procedures for greeting and serving guests, and attractiveness of the décor. Plus, there's a check of basic sanitation procedures, such as how food and dishware are handled.

Believing that Hugo deserved this after all he had done to get us up and running, I had another motive in encouraging him to accept the assignment. The inn to be inspected was a beautiful old plantation house with history. Shackles for slaves could still be seen attached to the basement walls, people said, because the house served as a stop on the Underground Railroad and fleeing slaves were confined at night. There were two reasons for this. One was to prevent a maverick from harming those who were sheltering them. The second was also to protect the homeowners: If a posse pursuing fleeing slaves came by, an owner could demonstrate that he had already captured them. I wanted Hugo to see this basement.

After a tour by the current owner, which did not include the basement, and the inspection, he ventured to ask about any Civil War history connected with the house. The period has not been well documented and preserved in our region and only lately have some important stations on the Underground Railroad been uncovered, discussed, and mapped out.

"There isn't any," she answered. "Absolutely none."

Hugo came home pleased with his new job of bed-and-breakfast inspector, even if some aspects of life here remained opaque, and probably always would.

I guess everything's set, I thought for the last time, with two solid years behind us. We've got the hang of this reinvented life. It's not easy for older dogs to learn new tricks but it looks like we somehow renewed a house, and ourselves along with it. The doctors pronounced Hugo's comeback miraculous. The catastrophe brought us closer than I could have dreamed. He still couldn't drive for more than an hour at a time, which meant I had to go along whenever he went to a doctor's office, to see his dad, or any distance at all. He still took a nap or two most days and he still forgot things like locking doors at night, closing his office window before a storm, paying bills on time—trivialities.

As for the bed-and-breakfast, bookings continued to flow in. The pain I got in my chest when money was tight let up. Each season after the first was busier than the one before, with tourists, weekenders, and brides-to-be booking for their guests, families, and sometimes themselves. Almost everyone is pleasant and fits the profile of the typical bed-and-breakfast guest: affluent, sophisticated, and seeking a pleasant alternative to the commercial hotel experience. Hotels and large inns have been trying to tap into the bed-and-breakfast market, but until they come up with truly personal service, freshly prepared meals with authentic ingredients and flavors, until they decorate with genuine furniture rather than made-for-hotels reproductions and plastic-lined curtains—the business, according to analysts, seems reasonably secure. Of course there are clouds on the horizon.

Guest expectations are on the rise. Once a bed-and-breakfast, a British invention, promised not much more than that, a concept that didn't flower on this side of the Atlantic. The traditional British bed-and-breakfast was, and is, a relatively inexpensive, no-frills form of accommodation, often with a bath shared with other guests and breakfast served at the host family's own table. In this country guests seek luxurious amenities and facilities. How thick are your towels? the newsletter of the national innkeeper association asks. What is the thread count of your sheets? How many courses do you offer for breakfast? Do you provide WiFi, computers, Jacuzzis, in-room telephones, voice mail, and flat-screen TV? Do you offer breakfast in the room as an alternative to the dreaded communal breakfast table? Do you have separate entrances for the guests? A pool, a sauna, a massage room? If not, the association advises, consider adding these and as many other luxuries as you can conjure.

Another cloud is the ever-increasing cost of the real estate necessary to house all this luxury. The *Wall Street Journal* calls the American bed-and-breakfast, as it has evolved, endangered. Unless you already happen to own the real estate, it now takes an establishment with many guest rooms, booked more than just seasonal weekends, to pay the bills. Ten rooms is the number often given. As the president of the Maryland Bed and Breakfast Association, Joseph Lespier, points out, the average length of bed and breakfast ownership is seven years; the average age of the innkeepers is over fifty-five; in Maryland more are going out of business than are opening up. "Do the math," he observes. "In ten years, at this rate, there won't be a significant number of bed-and-breakfasts left in Maryland."

Still, the bed-and-breakfast, with its invitation to escape into a more romantic, bygone era and relax over an inviting breakfast, has become an established tradition. More accurately, it is a group of traditions with bed-and-breakfasts as different as snowflakes, as individualistic as their hosts. There are bed-and-breakfasts with books, easy chairs, and reading lights. Others specialize in skiing, cooking classes, breadmaking, spa treatments, horseback riding, wine tasting, yoga, theater, ghosts, musicmaking, ballroom dancing, or murder mysteries. There are bed-and-breakfasts in vineyards and on flower farms and I visited one recently with a wolf protection program and some forty wolves in residence on the grounds. All manner of experience awaits enjoyment. If enforced conviviality isn't for you, just ask before booking at a particular bed-and-breakfast. Speaking with the owner or innkeeper is an excellent way to find out about the general ambience and determine if you will feel comfortable.

For the time being, I decided not to worry about the long-term implications of the business. We were fortunate to have enough guests coming our way to keep going, even without Jacuzzis and television. A neighbor stopped me as I came out of the post office and remarked on how much we've done for the village by fixing up the house and opening a business. Since we arrived, the closed-up general store became a café-restaurant. Other neighbors have put lights like ours in their windows. The latest newcomers, the ones from New York, got an all-out welcome from the neighborhood. The place is brighter, through the efforts of many. That's more than enough.

For the last time ever I think, *we're all set . . .*

It's the middle of September. I half-listen to a weather report on the radio before falling asleep. A hurricane is moving up the Atlantic Coast and predictions are that it may veer left and roar straight up the Chesapeake Bay. As far away as Washington, D.C., sandbags are being piled along the Potomac River.

Not directly on the bay, we expect heavy wind and rain— nothing to worry about. I fall into a peaceful sleep.

At dawn, Hugo shakes me awake. I know we have guests checking in, but I don't want to get up yet. He's hunched over, looking out the window.

He points down Royal Oak Road. "Look."

From the window as far as I can see before the road curves away toward the church, the road looks exactly the way it always does in the rain—shiny and black.

"No, look at the fire truck." With lights flashing, a fire truck moves silently past our driveway. The water, he points out, reaches almost to the top of the truck's huge wheels.

I look again, tear out of bed, and run downstairs. Stepping into duck boots and throwing a slicker over my nightgown, I rush outside. Hugo, in pajamas, follows.

Water, coming from I don't know where, laps the hubcaps of my car, which is parked near the bottom of the driveway. "Get the car keys," I yell, always better at giving orders than taking action. While he moves the car to higher ground, I try to make sense of what I see.

The road is definitely under a lot of water. In the dim light I make out that the spacious lawn across the way has vanished. The lower trunks of the old oaks and cedars are submerged in a lakeful of water. The garden bench and putting green are gone. Where the volleyball net used to be, I see the tops of two poles. Overnight we have become a waterfront property.

Not knowing what else to do, we go inside and fill pans with drinking water in case the power goes off, which means the well pump won't work. I hunt for candles and flashlight batteries while Hugo takes phone calls from the incoming guests, all canceling. The wedding has been moved to Baltimore.

The TV news reports that all roads around us are flooded. The Tilghman Island road is closed and Route 33 is under water at the Oak Creek Bridge. Even if we could get to the Bay Bridge, it too is closed because of high winds. We cannot go anywhere.

I recall the former owner's description of our house. "One of the prominent structures of Royal Oak," he wrote, "the house sits along a historic road, on high ground." The prominent structures presumably being our house and the falling-down church, I had to wonder what he meant by *high ground.*

Outside I take another look around and it crosses my mind that I'm about to find out. The rain has let up but the wind is wailing at thirty-five, maybe forty miles an hour. The ground doesn't look especially high around our house and in the side yard a pond has appeared, complete with three ducks.

Now with more light what I see is astonishing. It takes long minutes to comprehend the new landscape. In place of the road, a wide, shimmering canal stretches out of sight. The house diagonally across from us on the creek side is, unfortunately, completely surrounded by water, rising almost halfway up the front door.

In a canoe, neighbors paddle our way. High tide in two hours, they call out helpfully. Walking around to the front of our house, I see water lapping at the stone steps below the gate. I check my watch, realizing that everything we've tried to build here could all wash away before tomorrow.

A crack like gunfire interrupts my thoughts and I look up to see the old locust on the north side of the house crash down on the power line thirty feet from where I am standing.

The neighbors paddle away. If water reaches the porch steps, I decide we'll start rolling up the rugs.

With an hour to go, I station myself at the old iron gate to keep an eye on the tide as it advances in small muddy swirls, each swirl not especially dangerous-looking by itself, but each one lapping determinedly higher under the gate.

Okay, I say out loud to no one, *I finally get it.* You are not all set, you will never be all set, and you will never think like that again. The gods do not like it. That is why the wise talk about the universality of change. That is why your grandmother and your mother always said, "I'll be there, God willing, and the creek don't rise."

A few minutes before ten, with water licking the toes of my boots, I watch, hardly daring to breathe, as it stops rising; it just stops. In disbelief, I stare as the water touches the tips of my boots again and then again before it starts inching away.

Almost imperceptibly at first, it retreats. Over the next hours the receding water picks up speed, leaving a long tail of mud and debris, plastic bottles, strips of rubber tire, lumber, and soda cans, along with handfuls of pottery shards. A canal still flows where the street used to be and the lawn across the way is still a lake, but unmistakably the water is ebbing.

I keep watch for another half-hour to be sure it doesn't start rising again and to warn neighbors away from the downed power lines dangling in the water. Two young children row up the canal. As they climb out, smiling and splashing their way toward me, waist deep in the dark sinister-looking water, I shout at them to get away. In the wind they can't hear me. I wave my arms frantically until I see them climb back in their boat.

Hugo comes outside and we watch a weak sun break through the clouds. The wind lets up. We walk around checking for damage, looking up and down the canal for an electric company truck, not really expecting to see one unless they have an amphibious vehicle. A flicker of light from the deserted cottage on the other side of the fallen locust catches my eye and I turn in time to see an enormous white bird, head high, emerge from the doorway in ridiculous mincing steps.

It's a ptarmigan, Hugo says. With his medications and whatever rearrangement of his neural pathways has taken place, he now possesses the gift of an exotic vocabulary at the tip of his tongue. He seems surprised, almost dismissive, that I don't know what a ptarmigan is. A type of grouse, he explains, found in northern Canada. He spells it out. I flatly say I don't believe him.

The white bird hesitates outside the cottage door. With jerky movements of a long scrawny neck, it surveys the mucky, transformed landscape, the piles of detritus at its door, the new canal and the lake beyond. It takes a sidestep, then another, skittishly detouring around a downed tree limb. Noticing us, the bird stops short and I see ruffled feathers sticking straight out the top of its head that remind me of a peacock.

The bird retreats—I can't say for sure but my impression is that it can walk in reverse—to the cottage. Once we back off to our front porch, it reappears. Darting glances right and left, it advances with a few steps forward, a few back, more forward, until it crosses the ravine. Under the willow on our side of the ravine, the bird stops.

It is very white, I see now, and has unexpected brown eyes. Some of the white head feathers, like an off-kilter bridal wreath, are sadly broken or twisted. Fixing a long stare on us, the bird unfurls its tail in a great luminous crescent, casting an unworldly glow across the mud. Without a doubt a peacock, not too much the worse for the storm.

The next morning Hugo reported the amazing sighting to Roland when he stopped by to see if we were okay. Before Hugo could ask what peacocks eat, Roland said, "I know that old peacock!"

"You *do?*"

"Sure, I do. He lives in the woods back of my house."

A *white* peacock?

"Sure. He's been around a long time. Probably got away years ago from one of the big farms. Came down your way after the wind let up to see for himself what all the commotion was, the water rising and all that. Won't stay though."

"Even for food?"

"Nope. This one wants to be on his own. Won't stay unless you fence him in or clip his wings. My grandma kept peacocks and that's what you have to do—nip the wing feathers so they can't fly. Of course if you do that, then you have to watch out for foxes." Peacocks like corn, he said, and will go into a field after the harvest and eat all the corn kernels that are left.

I set out canned corn for the peacock, but didn't try to fence in this bizarre, roving symbol of—what? Curiosity? Adaptability? Endurance? Luck? Maybe all of these. The bird stayed in the boarded-up cottage, coming out twice a day to eat corn on our porch steps. After three days, when all the water was back in the creek, it left for good.

Home

OF COURSE OUR LITTLE BYWAY WILL CHANGE, IS
changing, and neither we nor the house will stay renewed.
A developer is proposing to construct a "faux marsh" up the
way so more housing can be set closer to the waterline. New
cracks are opening in ceilings we patched so carefully. Last
week a hawk almost got Annabelle.

At the same time, sensations and rhythms have imprint-
ed themselves. The scent of a freshly mown field, the first
sighting of the osprey pairs in spring, early summer calls of
the bob-white, the clammy smell of the late-summer creek,
the geese families arriving in fall, as you come to know the
land and water and anticipate the signs of change. The

search for renewal, for something more than the old life, all this says, worked.

It still didn't seem completely like home, though. Maybe you can't have both renewal and a comfortable at-home feeling, I reasoned, even after we built a bedroom addition onto the house and moved in for good in the fourth year. I can't remember exactly when I stopped saying it wasn't home.

It was sometime after I found, on the north side of the house where runaway bushes, wisteria, and brambles separate us from a line of tumbledown cottages, a patch of white-flowered mint. *Wild mint,* I said to no one. *I could make a julep if I like. There are no cultural police or ordinances to say you can't. You could make a julep and sit on the porch.*

Old French from the Persian, *gul* for rose and *ab* for water, *julep* means a syrup or sweetened liquid used in drinks or desserts. In English, an early reference is to a julep made of violets. This cooling drink is a traditional way to celebrate summer, I remembered reading in a history of local cooking at the library, a way, as a Marylander once expressed it, "for noble minds to travel together upon the flower-strewn paths of happy and congenial thought."

Just now the house is empty; new guests won't arrive until tomorrow. There's time, I tell myself. There *is* time. You could make a julep, sit on the porch, and rejoice that the path, not always happy, congenial, or flower-strewn by any stretch, led us here together. You could sit here and remember all the family, friends, and strangers who helped you along the way. And I did.

It was after that and after I walked down to Oak Creek, just visible from the porch, yet one more time that I stopped saying it wasn't home. Every day, every hour there is different. In the fall you might catch bronze or flame-orange reflections of shoreline trees. In February, a white-and-black symphony of frozen waves. On a still afternoon in shimmering heat, opaline water merges with sky. At sunset on an ordinary day the creek might suddenly turn into rainbow ice cream or a wide smoky pink-violet ribbon surrounded on all sides by dark blue.

You might glimpse a duet of dragonflies or barn swallows, ducks, swans, geese, gulls, a splash of fish, a snake gliding surreptitiously past that beautiful swimmer, the blue crab, or a hawk cruising for songbirds. In the distance, a white dot of sail tracing the horizon. Closer in, a workboat noisily patrolling for fish. At the shore, statue-still and silently fishing against a mural of high marsh grasses and mallows in flower, a blue heron, a great white egret, or a belted kingfisher. Overhead, a pair of acrobatic ospreys.

The fragrances of the creek, wild, tame, or an intoxicating blend, as brine mingles with grasses, marsh, diesel fumes, and the sounds rising from it all—wind, birds, and engines—join in a chant of purpose and message. When you walk down to the water's edge, there is no telling what you'll find.

Then, too, something changed about the house itself over time. She—houses like ships are indisputably feminine—is still beautiful, still restored, and lately flaunts a brass plaque attesting to her historic merit. Hopefully, this will give her a better chance at survival than when we first found her and I expect she will survive longer than we ourselves will. But something changed. Hugo no longer caresses a swath of plaster he's just repaired, lovingly checking to see if it's as perfect as can be. I no longer hunt for the ultimate house accessory. The recollection of tracking down the perfect doorknob for the parlor—slightly decorative but not too ornate, a reproduction rather than a costly original, but a careful, subdued one with just the right patina—makes me shake my head now in wonder.

Still as fine as the day we finished work, the house has faded in my day-to-day awareness to slightly blurred background. Walking through the rose, yellow, and cream rooms, I may be looking for Hugo. When he takes a nap, I wake him up after fifteen or twenty minutes to be sure he's all right, and probably always will.

The other day he admitted that at the start of this journey he was scared and unskilled. We're older now, he pointed out, and know more. If we ever move on, it won't be because this wasn't good, worthy, even wonderful. The reason would be that it isn't possible for us to think in large increments of time anymore. How would you like to spend the next thirty, twenty, or even ten years is a question for the young, not us. But home, yes, and so much sweeter because of the bitter.

The fields, too. Last autumn the back field turned entirely yellow again, not brilliant buttercup yellow this time, but a paler, softer, impossibly gold-orange-yellow. I walked out through the gate to see if the buttercups had come back and instead found soybean plants drying in the fall light. Without a doubt the scene was more beautiful than before. I picked my way slowly along the edge of the field, which was fringed with majestic goldenrod spires, small white daisies, a reprise of June's flowering chicory, and some newcomers. First I spotted tiny sky-blue morning glories twining up through the soybeans' teardrop leaves and almost missed a knockout of a flower, buttery with touches of blush on the outer petals and, at its center, exactly matching pink and yellow stamens. Three or four perched on a stem, they seemed like miniature butterflies. I stood perfectly still, letting the scene wash over me, symbolism and all, not wanting to think or analyze for once, just taking it all in.

Notes from the
Kitchen

❧

HERE IS A SAMPLING OF DISHES THAT HAVE WON THE hearts of our guests at Royal Oak House, and that at the same time are true to the spirit of the Chesapeake's Eastern Shore, its history, land, seasons, and farms.

Yes, there are no crabs here because this rarity, perfectly fresh crab, is really best savored on a special occasion close to the source, dockside, with a fork or mallet in hand. The recipes we've chosen to include for breakfast, teatime, and brunch draw on widely available—and unendangered— ingredients. They are mostly simple to prepare if you know your way around a kitchen, and a few, like the pears and maybe a succulent breakfast pudding, are easy even if you don't. Please enjoy!

FRUITS & FIRSTS

A Pair of Pears
Old-Fashioned Blackberry Muffins
Cloud Muffins

SWEETS

Sticky Buns As Big As Your Hand
Apple–Sour Cherry Crisp with Rebel Yell
Persimmon Pudding
Black Walnut Milk Cake
Hugo's Prizewinning Praline Pumpkin Pie

MAINS & SIDES

Eastern Shore Breakfast Pudding
Old Bay Potatoes
Bay Spice
Royal Oak Fried Chicken
Southern Green Beans
Green Tomatoes

ON THE PORCH

Mint Juleps

FRUITS & FIRSTS

. . .

A Pair of Pears

With citrus and star anise, these poached pears make a refreshing and eye-catching start to breakfast or brunch.

2 large, firm, ripe pears
1/2 lemon
2 cups water
1 tablespoon honey
4 star anise
1 teaspoon vanilla
2 tablespoons zest of lime*
2 tablespoons zest of orange
sweetened lime juice (or Rose's brand)
grenadine syrup

Cut the pears in half lengthwise, peel and remove the cores, leaving the stems for a decorative touch. In a medium-size, stainless steel saucepan, place the pears in a single layer, cut side down, and squeeze lemon juice over the fruit to prevent it from turning brown. Add water, honey, two of the star anise, and vanilla. Cover and simmer until fruit is fork tender, about 15 minutes.

Remove the pears to four small dessert plates, cut side down, decorating each plate with a star anise (which is beautiful but inedible—substitute an herb leaf or an edible flower if you prefer). Reduce juices if necessary to four tablespoons and pour the juice over the fruit. Sprinkle the zest of the citrus on each serving and pour a teaspoon of lime juice alongside each pear half and a teaspoon of grenadine syrup along the other side. Serves 4.

* Zest is the thinnest outer layer of green skin, either grated or sliced away from the bitter white pith beneath and finely chopped.

• • •

Old-Fashioned Blackberry Muffins

Crammed with berries, this light batter's only purpose is to hold all the fruit together.

> 2 cups flour
> 1/2 cup sugar
> 1/2 teaspoon salt
> 2 teaspoons baking powder
> 2 eggs, beaten
> 1/4 cup canola oil
> 3/4 cup milk
> 1 teaspoon vanilla
> 1/2 pound fresh blackberries or 3/4 pound frozen
>   berries, defrosted and well-drained. Red raspberries
>   are wonderful, too, or you can use a combination of
>   red and black berries, if you like.

Heat the oven to 400 degrees. Oil a 12-muffin tin and set it aside.

In a medium-sized mixing bowl stir together with a fork the flour, sugar, salt, and baking powder. In a second bowl, blend the eggs, oil, milk, and vanilla. Combine this mixture

quickly and lightly with the dry ingredients. The batter should be lumpy. Gently fold berries into the batter and spoon the batter into the tin, filling each cup two-thirds full.

Bake for 15 to 20 minutes, until the tops are light brown and the muffins are springy to the touch. Serve hot or slightly cool with a fresh berry and a mint leaf perched atop each muffin with a dab of honey. Makes 12 muffins.

• • •

Cloud Muffins

The more cream and butter, the more cloudlike the taste.

2 cups flour
1 tablespoon baking powder
1 teaspoon salt
1/8 teaspoon nutmeg, freshly grated
1 cup heavy cream
8 tablespoons butter, melted
2/3 cup sugar
2 eggs
1 teaspoon vanilla
1/4 pound fresh blackberries, or 1/3 pound frozen
　　berries, defrosted and well-drained

Heat the oven to 400 degrees. Butter a 12-muffin tin or line with paper muffin cups.

In a medium-sized mixing bowl whisk together the flour, baking powder, salt, and nutmeg. In a second bowl whisk together the cream, butter, sugar, eggs, and vanilla. Combine this mixture with the dry ingredients, taking care not to over-mix. Fold in berries. Divide the batter among the muffin cups. Bake until a toothpick comes out clean, about 12 to 15 minutes. Serve warm. Makes 12 muffins.

SWEETS

. . .

Sticky Buns As Big As Your Hand

The cooks at the Pasadena Inn in Royal Oak baked sticky buns "as big as your hand," remembers a long-time resident who was lucky enough to eat them. "They smelled so good you just about couldn't stand it." In the 1920s this inn was home to the cast and crew for the filming of Gary Cooper's *The First Kiss*. Judged "impossible and overdrawn," the film does not survive, but memory of the sticky buns lives on.

FOR THE DOUGH

1/2 cup milk
3 tablespoons oil or butter
3 tablespoons sugar
1/2 teaspoon salt
1/2 cup water
1 egg, beaten
3 1/2 cups flour, plus 1/2 cup
2 teaspoons yeast

FOR THE FILLING

1 cup dark brown sugar, packed
4 teaspoons cinnamon
1/8 teaspoon each, cloves and nutmeg
3/4 cup raisins

FOR THE TOPPING

3/4 cup dark brown sugar, packed
3 tablespoons butter
1 tablespoon corn syrup
3/4 cup pecan pieces

Heat the milk in a saucepan to just under a simmer, then remove from heat and add 3 tablespoons oil or butter, sugar, and salt. Stir and pour into a large mixing bowl. Add the water to cool the milk. Blend in the egg, 3 to 3 1/2 cups flour, and yeast, stirring until the dough pulls away from the bowl. If it's sticky, work in more flour until you can gather the dough into a ball. Rub the dough ball lightly with oil and return it to the bowl. Cover with plastic wrap or a damp dish towel and set it in a warm place (75–90 degrees) until the dough doubles in size, about 1 1/2 to 2 hours. Punch down the dough and allow it to rest for 30 minutes, covered as before.

For the filling, combine the sugar, cinnamon, cloves, nutmeg, and raisins and set aside.

For the topping, stir together in a small saucepan the sugar, butter, and corn syrup over low heat until just melted (or heat in the microwave for one minute).

Thickly butter a 9 x 13 inch baking pan and pour the topping mix, along with the pecans, into the pan, distributing evenly.

Roll out the dough to a large rectangle, approximately 12 x 20 inches, and spread the filling over the surface. Starting on the short side of the rectangle, roll up the dough to enclose the filling, and cut six slices across the roll.

Place the rolls in the pan and press with the palm of your hand to even and flatten them slightly. Cover loosely until they have doubled in size, about an hour. Shortly before this second rise is complete, heat the oven to 350 degrees. Uncover the rolls and bake on the middle oven rack for 25 to 28 minutes, or until the tops turn medium brown. With a knife immediately loosen the hot rolls from the sides of the pan and invert onto a platter. If you can, keep everyone away until the sticky buns have cooled. Very generously serves 6.

· · ·

Apple-Sour Cherry Crisp with Rebel Yell

The tartness of lightly sugared fruits complements bourbon-flavored whipped cream and provides a pleasing start or finish to a festive breakfast.

FOR THE CRISP
4 medium apples, about 1 3/4 pounds, peeled, cored, and thinly sliced*
3/4 pound sour cherries, pitted, or one 14-ounce can tart cherries packed in water, well drained
1 cup flour, half whole wheat pastry flour and half-white flour

1/4 cup oats
8 tablespoons butter
1/2 cup brown or white sugar,
    plus 2 tablespoons for the cherries
1 teaspoon cinnamon
1/2 teaspoon allspice
pinch of salt
1/3 cup walnuts, coarsely chopped

FOR THE CREAM
1/2 pint heavy cream
1 tablespoon white sugar
1 tablespoon bourbon, such as Rebel Yell

Heat the oven to 375 degrees. Butter an 8 x 8 baking dish. Stir 2 tablespoons of sugar into the cherries, then place all the fruit in the baking dish. In a bowl blend the flour, oats, butter, remaining sugar, cinnamon, allspice, and salt with a fork, pastry cutter, or your fingers until it looks like lumpy bread crumbs. Stir in the nuts. Spread the mixture on top of the fruit. Bake for 30 to 35 minutes, until the topping is lightly browned and the fruit bubbles gently around the edges.

Whip together the cream and sugar until it holds soft peaks. Stir in the bourbon. Serve the fruit crisp hot or warm with spoonfuls of cream on top and pass the Rebel Yell for those who want to have a little fruit with their bourbon. Serves 5.

* *Granny Smith apples retain their shape after baking, as does a combination with a softer apple, such as Macintosh, which adds juice. We like Golden Delicious, which offers both flavor and texture.*

. . .

Persimmon Pudding

Native persimmons ripen to red-orange in the fall. Favored by Native Americans and early colonists for bread and pudding, persimmons taste uniquely of apricot, peach, and pumpkin.

2 cups persimmon pulp*
2 eggs, beaten
1/3 cup maple syrup
1 3/4 cups buttermilk
1/4 cup canola oil
2 cups flour
1 teaspoon baking soda
1 teaspoon cinnamon
1 teaspoon ginger
1/4 teaspoon nutmeg
1 teaspoon vanilla
Pinch of salt

OPTIONAL FOR SERVING
Cream sweetened with sugar and a dash of vanilla
Crystallized ginger, finely minced

Heat the oven to 350 degrees. Butter a shallow 9 x 12 inch, nonreactive baking dish (such as glass or enamel). In a large mixing bowl, combine persimmon pulp, eggs, and all remaining ingredients, and stir until well blended.

Pour the batter into the dish and bake for 55 to 60 minutes, until the center is set. Spoon into warm bowls and serve with cream or whipped cream, sweetened with a tablespoon of sugar and a teaspoon of vanilla. Finely minced crystallized ginger on top of the pudding or the whipped cream adds sparkle. This is comfort food. Serves 8.

Note: Persimmons are a fruit that inspires yearning. If you must have true American persimmon pudding out of season, Dillman Farm will airship the frozen pulp to you, at a price: 800-359-1362 or Dillmanfarm.com

Persimmons must be completely ripe, soft, and juicy for use. If preparing fresh persimmons, discard seeds and press fruit through a sieve or purée in a food processor. If using canned, sweetened persimmon pulp, omit the maple syrup.

• • •

Black Walnut Milk Cake

The fragrance and piquance of American black walnuts infuse this homey vanilla cake, baked in a cast-iron pan.

4 eggs
1 cup sugar
2 cups flour
2 teaspoons baking powder
pinch of salt
1/4 pound butter, melted
1 cup milk
2 teaspoons vanilla
3/4 cup chopped black walnuts
1/4 cup powdered sugar, as garnish

Heat the oven to 375 degrees. Lightly butter and flour a 10-inch cast-iron, ovenproof frying pan.

Separate egg yolks from the whites and set the yolks aside. In a mixing bowl, beat the egg whites until they hold soft peaks. In another bowl, beat together the sugar and egg yolks until the mixture turns creamy and lemon-colored. In a third, larger bowl, whisk together the flour, baking powder, and salt, and then add the sugar-egg yolk mixture, along with the melted butter, milk, and vanilla, blending until smooth. Fold in the egg whites and walnuts.

Pour the batter into the pan and bake for about 40 minutes, until the cake turns golden and a toothpick inserted in the center comes out clean. Delectable warm or cool, dusted with powdered sugar. Serves 8 to 10.

· · ·

Hugo's Prizewinning Praline Pumpkin Pie

What does it take to turn out a prizewinning pie? Lots of "mouth feel," as the saying goes. When the pie cracked as it baked, we added a last-minute ring of pecan praline and that convenient coverall, a small mountain of brandy whipped cream, for first prize in the St. Michaels contest, restaurant division.

9-inch deep-dish pie shell

FOR THE FILLING
1 15-ounce can pumpkin, unsweetened
1 cup brown sugar, loosely packed

2 teaspoons cinnamon*
1/4 teaspoon cloves*
2 teaspoons fresh ginger, grated
1/4 teaspoon salt
2/3 cup whipping cream
2/3 cup milk
4 eggs

FOR THE PRALINE
3 tablespoons flour
3 tablespoons brown sugar
2 tablespoons butter, softened
3/4 cup pecan halves

FOR THE CREAM
1/2 pint whipping cream
1 tablespoon sugar
1 tablespoon brandy

Heat the oven to 400 degrees. Partly bake the pie shell on the middle oven rack for about 10 minutes until it looks set.

In a food processor, blend the pumpkin, sugar, spices, and salt for one minute. In a heavy saucepan, cook this pumpkin mixture at a simmer, stirring constantly, for about 5 minutes.

Remove pumpkin from the heat and stir in the cream and milk. Whisk eggs to combine whites and yolks and blend thoroughly into the pumpkin mixture. Pour this into the pie shell, adding any extra filling after the pie has baked for about 5 minutes.

Bake the pie on the lower oven rack for about 20 minutes

and prepare the praline. In a small bowl, combine the flour, sugar, and butter and stir in the pecans. Remove the pie from the oven and spoon the pecan mixture in a circle around the edge of the pie, inside the crust, and return it to the oven. Continue baking for about 10 minutes more until the filling is puffed and wiggles very slightly when the pie is gently shaken. Cool on a wire rack.

Whip the cream and sugar together until stiff, then stir in the brandy. When the pie is completely cool, mound the cream on top, inside the ring of pecans. Serve right away or refrigerate. Serves 6 to 8.

*Freshly ground cinnamon and cloves are best, but spice straight from the jar will do.

MAINS & SIDES

...

Eastern Shore Breakfast Pudding

Eggs, cheddar, ham or sausage, and bread baked together in the rich tradition of English savory puddings. This rib-sticking main course is equally delicious in a vegetarian rendition.

4 thick slices white bread, torn into quarters
3/4 pound cooked ham, thinly sliced and chopped
   (or 1 pound sausage meat, cooked and drained)

1 cup sharp cheddar cheese, grated
1/2 medium onion, minced
1 sweet red pepper, diced
1 tablespoon olive oil
6 eggs
2 cups milk
1/4 teaspoon salt
Black and red pepper to taste
Pinch of nutmeg
Parsley to garnish

Heat the oven to 350 degrees. Butter a deep 8 x 8 inch baking dish. Lay bread in the dish, covering the bottom, and top with the ham or sausage and cheese. In a small pan, sauté the onion and red pepper in oil until fragrant and softened, about 5 minutes, and layer on top of the cheese. Whisk together the eggs and milk, salt, peppers, and nutmeg. Pour the mixture over the bread, meat, vegetables, and cheese.

Bake for about one hour, until the pudding is puffed, firm, and golden brown. Tent with foil if necessary to prevent too much browning.

Cut into four squares, garnish with parsley, and serve along with Old Bay potatoes (below), steamed asparagus, and broiled tomatoes. You shouldn't see a hungry guest again until dinnertime.

Note: For vegetarians, substitute for the meat a cup each of lightly steamed broccoli cut into small florets and thinly sliced, sautéed zucchini—both well drained. Serves 4.

• • •

Old Bay Potatoes

A zesty take on home fries.

> 1 pound red-skinned potatoes
> 1/4 cup Bay Spice*
> 1/4 cup canola oil
> salt and pepper

Boil the potatoes, covered, in a pot of salted water until a knife easily pierces the potatoes but they are still firm, about 20 to 30 minutes. Drain and cool or refrigerate overnight. Cut the potatoes into halves or quarters, making 1-inch pieces. Pour the Bay Spice into a shallow dish and dredge the potatoes to coat them.

Heat oil in a medium-size frying pan, add potatoes, and cook, turning until all sides are brown, about 10 minutes. Add salt and pepper to taste. Serves 4.

Old Bay Seasoning can be purchased or you can make your own, as below.

• • •

Bay Spice

You can easily mix up Bay Spice yourself, since the McCormick Company generously gives the ingredients for its classic on the side of the box. The proportions are ours.

Stir together 1 tablespoon coarse salt with the following ground spices: 2 teaspoons paprika, 1/8 teaspoon cloves, and 1 teaspoon each of allspice, bay laurel, black pepper, cayenne pepper, cardamom, celery seed, ginger, mace, and mustard seed. It tastes even better if you grind the whole spices yourself.

. . .

Royal Oak Fried Chicken

According to legend, the aroma from the frying pans in which Royal Oak pullets were "assuming a beautiful brown" drew the British into St. Michaels, during the War of 1812 and "as part of the investigation," they shelled the town. From *Tales of Old Maryland,* by J.H.K. Shannahan Jr., 1907.

    1 chicken, about 3 pounds, cut into 8 pieces
    4 cups buttermilk
    1 cup flour
    1 teaspoon salt
    1 teaspoon black pepper
    1 cup canola oil

Wash and pat dry the chicken pieces and place them in a large bowl. Pour buttermilk over the chicken, cover, and refrigerate for 8 hours to overnight. In a shallow bowl, mix together flour, salt, and pepper. Remove chicken from the buttermilk and dredge the pieces in the flour mixture. Pat firmly to remove any extra flour.

Heat the oil in a large cast-iron pan until hot, but not smoking. Place chicken pieces skin side down, 3 or 4 at a time, in the oil. Cook about 10 minutes on a side, until the chicken turns golden brown and is cooked through. Remove to paper towels to drain. Serve warm or at room temperature with Southern green beans, below, and cornbread. Serves 4.

• • •

Southern Green Beans

Southerners will cry over vegetables cooked the traditional way. Susie, the best of friends, shared the secret.

6 slices bacon, cut in 2-inch strips
2 onions, sliced
1 pound green beans, stems removed
salt and pepper to taste
2 tablespoons sugar

OPTIONAL
1 cup diced potatoes and 1 cup corn kernels

Sauté the bacon and onions in a large saucepan until the bacon is crisp. Drain away fat, if you wish. Add the beans, season with salt and pepper, and cover with water. Simmer, covered, for a long time, 1 to 2 hours, depending how much patience you have.

Add the sugar, optional potatoes and corn, and simmer 30 minutes more. Serves 4 to 6.

• • •

Green Tomatoes

Green tomatoes have a beautiful lemony overtone. If you don't see them at a farmers market, ask because sometimes they're just being kept out of sight until they ripen. If you can't get green tomatoes, very firm red ones cooked this way are also tasty.

    4 medium-sized green tomatoes, sliced 1/4 inch thick,
        cores discarded
    1 tablespoon sugar
    salt and pepper to taste
    1/3 cup cornmeal
    1/3 cup flour
    1/2 cup canola oil

Sprinkle sugar, salt, and pepper over tomato slices. In a shallow dish, stir together the cornmeal, flour, more salt and pepper, and dredge the tomatoes. Press the coating firmly to the tomatoes. Heat 1/4 cup oil in a skillet and when hot but not smoking, add the slices a few at a time. Cook about 3 minutes on each side, until a golden-brown crust forms and the tomatoes are slightly softened and juicy. Add more oil to the pan as needed to fry the remaining tomatoes. Wonderful with eggs, ham, and toast. Serves 4.

ON THE PORCH

. . .

Mint Juleps

All you need for this traditional Southern emblem of hospitality is a handful of fresh mint, spirits, sugar, ice, and friends to share it.

4 teaspoons superfine or confectioner's sugar,
     plus extra to taste
20 mint sprigs, tough stems removed
water
finely crushed ice
bourbon or rye

In a shallow dish, mash the leaves of 16 mint sprigs with a spoon and combine with the sugar. Divide the mint sugar among 4 eight-ounce glasses—tall, narrow ones if you have them. Add enough water to cover the sugar and stir. Pour in a couple of ounces of the spirits until the glass is about a quarter full. You can stir in a little extra sugar now if you like. Fill the glasses to the top with crushed ice and decorate with the remaining mint. Stir again and serve. Happy thoughts!

Eight Good Reasons to Start a Bed-and-Breakfast and Seven Bad Ones

◆◌

OF ALL THE REASONS PEOPLE GIVE FOR WANTING TO START a bed-and-breakfast or acquire an existing one, few will hold up over time.

If your current job is running you into the ground and you long for a career change to make life easier, it is better to avoid the hospitality industry. If you enjoy socializing and expect that running a bed-and-breakfast will be an unending party with like-minded guests, the way the glossy magazine ads tell it, disappointment awaits you. If you're retiring and want a little something to do, you'll find yourself far busier than you ever intended, unless of course all you hope for is to rent out an extra room for occasional companionship. Even here, you could be in for disappointment because many guests will prefer to be left alone.

There are enticing reasons to persevere and if they speak to you, a bed-and-breakfast could be the right move.

EIGHT GOOD REASONS

Lifestyle

This is the chief reason many satisfied bed-and-breakfast owners cite for getting into the business. With two partners living and working together rather than traveling to jobs in different directions on different schedules, you can lead a more organic existence, a life closer to home. If, for example, you grow herbs and flowers for the guests, you can enjoy them, too. In other words, you get to spend time together in a setting that you would choose for vacation.

Money

Another good reason for going ahead. Instead of just sitting there, your house makes money for you. There can also be tax benefits to starting and running a bed-and-breakfast. Opportunities still exist, as well, to find a fixer-upper bargain in a town that has not yet turned around and develop it into a bed-and-breakfast. The opening of a bed-and-breakfast can be one of the first signs of an area's revitalization.

A Green Business

With the majority of bed-and-breakfasts housed in buildings over seventy-five years old, this can be the means to save a historic home from demolition. According to Jay Karen, president of the Professional Association of Innkeepers International, studies show that bed-and-breakfasts are a leading source for the preservation of historic houses in this country. If the structure requires modernization to the heating, electrical, and other systems, there are additional opportunities to benefit the environment and decrease the structure's carbon footprint. If period furnishings are part of the plan, further green savings are possible when you purchase used or antique furniture.

Be the Boss

You are in charge, you set the tone, decide when and how you will work, and when you will take time off.

Share Treasured Recipes

The opportunity to share what you do well can be a surprise benefit of the bed-and-breakfast business. Consider the cooking that your family and friends take for granted—a whole new audience awaits.

Show Off Your Decorating Skills

Here, too, many people will see and enjoy the results of your work. Equipping and decorating a bed-and-breakfast also offers a great excuse to shop for antiques and visit yard sales and auctions. Now it's a valid business activity.

Meet Interesting People

Bed-and-breakfasts generally self-select educated, affluent, and discerning guests. Many of them say they just want a nicer place to stay, a more refined experience, more accommodating of the individual and more interesting than a commercial hotel. These tend to be interesting people themselves and people with pleasing social skills.

Learn New Things

This may be the best of all reasons to run a bed-and-breakfast. With a variety of guests passing through your doors, it would be almost impossible not to learn something from almost everyone. A boat captain, noticing the heat from our commercial range, showed Hugo how to shut it down and light it as needed, the way they do on boats. A contractor explained how to insulate the inaccessible eaves of an old house. A visitor from South Carolina suggested jasmine for the garden because it thrives in summer heat and humidity. Other guests discovered an eating place open after all the restaurants have closed, where the food is excellent. A potter noticed the clay soil around our garage and asked if he could take some home. We gave him plastic bags, he shoveled up chunks of the clay, wet them down with the garden hose, and departed. Next thing I knew, a package arrived containing two small bowls, glazed deep blue and green on the rims, with the natural, unadorned clay showing below. An English professor gave us an informative volume of essays about the bay. One morning after breakfast, two dance instructors taught everyone the rudiments of the rumba.

On the purely practical side, running a business like this teaches efficiencies of planning and time management that make "normal" life easier. A formal, three-course breakfast for twelve? No problem. A garden scheme for the walkways that looks good all year—simple. Pansies bloom in our climate from fall to spring and begonias from spring to fall. In the past I worked ten times harder in the garden with a lot less to show for it: Now it was necessary to discover what would contribute to a dependable, pleasing ambience with minimal labor and expense.

AND SEVEN BAD ONES

Reasons why you should *not* start or acquire a bed-and-breakfast are the other face of the very reasons for going forward.

Lifestyle

Leading a work life closer to home means that the stresses can spill over into your private life, with work becoming the only, and seemingly inescapable, reality. Burnout is high. Everyone in the business for any length of time emphasizes the importance of taking breaks away from the workplace, especially if you live at the bed-and-breakfast, which is a requirement in some areas for licensing.

Among those who open a bed-and-breakfast, approximately a third leave by five years, another third are out of business by ten years, and a committed third last for twenty years or longer. The average length of bed-and-breakfast ownership is seven years.

Money

Yes, your house as a bed-and-breakfast will bring in money, but the high cost of real estate means it is harder than in the past to make a go of a bed-and-breakfast. It used to be estimated that you needed five rooms to "make money," including living expenses and paying a mortgage. Now the figure more often given is ten rooms, depending on the surroundings, competition, and overall economy of the region where your B&B is situated.

Every day hundreds of bed-and-breakfasts are offered for sale, typically ranging from about $300,000 for a small one in northern Michigan to a bed-and-breakfast with seven rooms in prime Vermont tourist territory for $1.3 million. In New York the range is even greater and you can find wide choice all over the country from $800,000 to $2 million.

The average price charged per night for a room at a bed-and-breakfast in this country is $144, according to the Professional Association of Innkeepers International. With many amenities and a highly desirable resort setting, rooms at a smaller number of establishments, as for example on Martha's Vineyard or the California coast, can run as much as $300 to $400 a night. Even at that level, the arithmetic is sobering. How many nights a year will you have to rent the rooms to pay your bills?

Be the Boss

Yes, you are the boss but only up to a point. It can be a challenge to meet guests' expectations and highly demanding guests can push you to your limit if you let them. There is technique and art to determining when to say yes or no, and how to say it. When a family of five shows up on your doorstep in a late-night storm, will you squeeze three extra guests into a room they reserved for two? Will you serve coffee at four-thirty in the morning for a guest who likes coffee then? Will you grant a partial refund to someone who passes up breakfast? No, we learned to answer this question. Breakfast is a courtesy that accompanies the room.

Over time any chink in your policies will be detected and challenged. Long after we thought we had heard it all came a request to serve breakfast at midnight and another guest asking if his son, who was being married nearby, could come over with the groomsmen to dress for the wedding. All right, we said, never guessing that they would take over the parlor and front porch, to the great amusement of the neighbors. At the post office the next day, Hugo had some explaining to do. "We saw your front porch filled up with half-naked men," Francine commented. "*What* was going on?"

A colleague in Arizona had a guest who came to breakfast dressed in a jaw-dropping nightgown, one problem we haven't encountered yet. When a guest did ask not long ago if she could come down to breakfast in her pajamas, I agreed because there were no other guests staying that night. In the morning she turned up in heavy flannel pajamas decorated with teddy bears, more presentable than some in their street clothes.

Share Treasured Recipes

Many will appreciate your finest; a few won't. Some will request breakfast and leave it untouched. Some will have dietary restrictions, which is fine if you're told in advance, impossibly rude if you're informed as you are serving. People with restrictions generally know that asking in advance for a special meal helps ensure that they will get it. Those few guests who might come your way with a political agenda about food will try your patience.

Show Off Your Decorating Skills

Your antique beds may be authentic beauties, but they won't satisfy some guests' standards for size. "Do you mean an old-fashioned double bed like our grandparents slept in?" one caller asked. Almost everyone who books a room inquires about the bed. Some of those who require a king bed will settle for a queen and those who prefer a queen will settle for an old-fashioned double, but in our experience, the king people will never accept a double. Personal taste might have to bend to guest comfort if you want happy guests, or guests at all.

Meet Interesting People

. . . except when they are irascible or impossibly demanding. Then you are stuck counting the hours until they check out. When you open your doors to the public, you open the doors to many kinds of people.

Learn New Things

Yes, but there are things you don't want to learn and will anyway. That nice couple who stayed last weekend? They tried to flush a box of Swiss chocolates down the toilet.

IF YOU DECIDE
TO GO AHEAD ANYWAY

Most people go into the bed-and-breakfast business for the lifestyle and the economics and most leave it for the same reasons. Here are some points to keep in mind:

1. Expenses and Income. Estimate your expenses and the income to be generated by the bed-and-breakfast realistically to be sure you can cover your costs. These might include a mortgage and living costs, such as health insurance and savings for retirement, items that tend to be overlooked in a casual assessment. Couples who go into the bed-and-breakfast business commonly keep one person employed elsewhere to ensure a steady income flow, at least initially.

2. "Room Nights." A key factor in the income equation is how many nights you can expect to book your rooms year-round, not just in high season. This is based on the desirability of your place and the surroundings, as well as on how other similar establishments are faring in the vicinity of your bed-and-breakfast. Bear in mind that bed-and-breakfasts average a 40 percent occupancy rate.

3. Room Value. The related question of what you can charge for your rooms and services requires careful evaluation. Room rates typically vary from under $100 a night to $200 and up. Just because you think your inn is exquisitely charming and ought to be expensive, the competition might be intense or the overall economy of the area may price you out of the market. Research is necessary to set prices.

4. Marketing and Promotion. How effectively you will be able to promote your business may be difficult to assess at the outset. It requires skill and can be the source of expensive mistakes. If you previously ran a small business, or a large one, that experience will come in very handy.

5. Your Disposition and Skills. Are you flexible, do you have a calm disposition, and are you willing to work hard at the variety of jobs, some of them tedious and repetitive, that will need doing? If it will be a larger bed-and-breakfast, are you an effective manager of staff, skillful with budgets, accounting practices, and basic business strategies?

6. Personal Goals. Understand what you hope to gain personally from the experience. That is, determine your objective. Consider these: companionship, with a room or two booked now and then to bring people into the house; a hobby, meaning you aren't planning to support yourself on the income; or a moneymaking venture. Be candid.

7. Wise First Steps. Attend one of the seminars offered to aspiring innkeepers, such as those sponsored by the Professional Association of Innkeepers International (www.paii.org). This organization welcomes innkeepers-to-be as well as owners and managers of bed-and-breakfasts and country inns, and the association publishes an informative newsletter, *Innkeeping*. An exhaustive, nuts-and-bolts guidebook, *So—You Want to Be An Innkeeper,* discusses every aspect of the business and problems of innkeeping, from legal structures to risk management to market trends to equipping a "luxury" bathroom.

We took none of those wise steps. Had we attended a workshop or read that guidebook, I am sure we never would have opened a bed-and-breakfast, so daunting can the details seem in the aggregate, and we would have missed a great run. What we did was to visit a lot of bed-and-breakfasts and if you, like us, see fit to proceed mainly on exuberance with skills carried over from other businesses, and are game to learn from your mistakes, I suggest this at the very least.

Presumably, you are already familiar with, and enjoy, bed-and-breakfasts as a visitor, but try staying at a variety of establishments as you consider them now from an owner's perspective. The view is very different. Running a good bed-and-breakfast takes a certain frame of mind: You have to want to make people feel happy, comfortable, and welcomed at your place. As a guest you can sense this from the minute you arrive.

Sources

Prologue

Barth, John. "A Floating Aria," *Talking Tidewater: Writers on the Chesapeake*, edited by Richard Harwood. Chestertown, MD: Literary House Press, Washington College, 1996, 2003.

Emery, Theo. "After Steps to Desegregate, Plaintiffs Drop Tennessee Suit." *New York Times*, September 12, 2006. www.nyt.com.

Chapter 1 A Curious Ballast

Marcus Aurelius, *Selections from the Meditations of Marcus Aurelius,* translation and introduction by Benjamin E. Smith. New York: Century Company, 1899.

Chapter 2 Royal Oak

Chapelle, Suzanne Ellery, and Glenn O. Phillips. *African American Leaders of Maryland: A Portrait Gallery*. Baltimore: Maryland Historical Society, 2004.

Chesapeake Bay Maritime Museum. *From a Lighthouse Window: Recipes and Recollections from the Chesapeake Bay Maritime Museum*. St. Michaels, MD: Chesapeake Bay Maritime Museum, 1989.

Commager, Henry Steele, ed. *The Blue and the Gray: The Story of the Civil War as Told by Participants,* vol. 1. New York: Bobbs-Merrill Company, 1950.

Hallman, E.C. *The Garden of Methodism*. Peninsula Annual Conference of the Methodist Church, n.p., n.d.

Leonard, R. Bernice. *Twig and Turf,* vol. 3, *The Royal Oak*. St. Michaels, MD: privately printed, 1985.

Mariners' Museum, "Waters of Despair, Waters of Hope: African Americans on the Chesapeake," exhibition at the Chesapeake Bay Maritime Museum, St. Michaels, MD, on loan from the Mariners' Museum, Newport News, VA, spring 2007.

Preston, Dickson J. *Talbot County: A History.* Centreville, MD: Tidewater Publishers, 1983.

Public Broadcasting Service. "Africans in America: Frederick Douglass." June 28, 2007. www.pbs.org.

Shannahan, J.H.K. *Tales of Old Maryland: History and Romance on the Eastern Shore of Maryland.* Baltimore: Meyer and Thalheimer, 1907.

Chapter 6 The Bay

Baker, William C. "Averting a Chesapeake Disaster." *Washington Post* (November 2, 2008): B8.

Chesapeake Bay Foundation. "Susquehanna River Named America's Most Endangered River for 2005." April 20, 2005. www.cbf.org.

Chesapeake Bay Maritime Museum. "At Play on the Bay," a guide to the exhibit. St. Michaels, MD: Chesapeake Bay Maritime Museum, n.d.

Chesapeake Bay Program Office. "American Oyster." April 20, 2005. www.chesapeakebay.net.

Fahrenthold, David A. "Oyster Project Consumed with Problems: Predators Eat Test Shellfish." *Washington Post* (August 25, 2004): B2.

_____. "Pollution Rising in Tributaries of Bay, Data Show." *Washington Post* (December 5, 2007): B2.

_____. "To Some Chesapeake Crabbers, a $50 Document Is Priceless." *Washington Post* (August 24, 2009): A6.

Harp, David, and Horton, Tom. *Water's Way: Life Along the Chesapeake.* n.p. Elliott and Clark, 1992.

Horton, Tom, and Harp, David. "Living on the Edge—Man, Nature and the Chesapeake Bay," Lecture at the Avalon Theater, Easton, MD, January 9, 2008.

Trade Environment Database (TED) Case Studies. "The Blue Crab: A Declining Resource." April 20, 2005. www.american.edu/projects.

Warner, William W. *Beautiful Swimmers: Watermen, Crabs, and the Chesapeake Bay.* Boston: Little, Brown and Company, 1976.

Chapter 7 Family, Family
Eron, Carol. "James Michener: Life and Literature, American Style." *Washington Post* (September 19, 1976): F1.
Kilborn, Peter T. "Weekends with the President's Men." *New York Times* (June 30, 2006): D1.

Chapter 18 Coyote Dreams
Brazos River Rattlesnake Ranch. "Cottonmouth Water Moccasin." January 22, 2007. www.wf.net.
DesertUSA. "The Coyote: Canis latrans." November 6, 2006. www.desertusa.com.
Maryland State Department of Natural Resources. "Coyotes." July 23, 2006. www.dnr.state.md.us.

Chapter 19 Kitchen, Garden, Field
Cox, Beverly, and Martin Jacobs. *Spirit of the Harvest: North American Indian Cooking.* New York: Stewart, Tabori and Chang, 1991.

Chapter 20 As Simple As It Seems
Harwood, Richard, ed. *Talking Tidewater: Writers on the Chesapeake.* Chestertown, MD: Literary House Press, Washington College, 1996, 2003.

Chapter 21 Guests and Geese
"Conviction of Wife in Killing of Spouse Is Upheld." *Baltimore Sun* (September 28, 2000): 4B.
"Got Ghosts? Share Them with Us." *Star Democrat,* Easton, MD: October 20, 2005, www.stardem.com
Terrer, John. *Audubon Society Encyclopedia of North American Birds.* New York: Alfred A. Knopf, 1980.

Chapter 23 And the Creek Don't Rise
Carroll, Bill. "Demand Management: Beyond Yield Management." *Innkeeping,* Professional Association of Innkeepers International, 24, no. 12 (December 2006): 1.
Dougherty, Conor. "The Endangered B & B." *Wall Street Journal* (August 11, 2006): W1.

Chapter 24 Home

Hammond-Harwood House Association. *Maryland's Way: As Told by a Collection of Traditional Receipts Selected from Three Centuries of Maryland Cooking*. Annapolis: Hammond-Harwood House Association, 1963.

Jones, Beth. "What's Not to Love About a Marsh?" *Water's Edge*. St. Michaels, MD: Bay Hundred Foundation Newsletter, May 2007.

Eight Good Reasons to Start a Bed-and-Breakfast and Seven Bad Ones

Brown, Susan et al. *So—You Want to Be an Innkeeper: The Definitive Guide to Operating a Successful Bed-and-Breakfast or Country Inn*. San Francisco: Chronicle Books, 2004.

Professional Association of Innkeepers International, www.paii.org.

Acknowledgments

◗ঙ

I wish to thank all those named and unnamed here for providing ideas, insight, and help in many different ways.

At the Historical Society of Talbot County, Beth Hansen led me to a trove of information on the region, as did Scotti Oliver at the Talbot County Library, along with the staff of the library's Maryland Room, Beth Jones at the Bay Hundred Foundation, and Captain Wade Murphy. Pete Lesher, curator of the Chesapeake Bay Maritime Museum, expertly reviewed historical portions of the book, for which I am very grateful. Naturalist Tom Horton gave inspiration through his writings about the Chesapeake Bay, as did Helen Chappell in hers and in conversation. William Habig drew my attention to attitudes toward emancipation in Maryland, the state where Frederick Douglass and Harriet Tubman were born, a state that solidly supported Barack Obama in the 2008 presidential election, the same state where OBAMA FOR PRESIDENT signs were burned.

Those who encouraged this project from the beginning include Margaret Bauer, Karen Binswanger, Dianne Stephens, Rita Geier, Keven Wilder, Amy Taylor, and Jean and Gary

Ratner, true friends. Also Robert and Kathy Day, Theron Raines, and John Nicoll. Brigitte Weeks kindly read an early draft and offered hope. Gail Greco, who celebrates bed-and-breakfasts in her many books, made useful comments, as did Jay Karen, president of the Professional Association of Innkeepers International, who generously took time to read the entire manuscript.

Thanks to everyone who shared their stories about the bed-and-breakfast life, including the hosts at over a hundred of these remarkable establishments, which Hugo and I visited before embarking on our own adventure. Especially Hugh and Jeannie Taylor of the Outermost Inn, Martha's Vineyard; Joe and Raquel Sanchez of the Aspen Inn, Flagstaff, Arizona; and Vicki Barrett at Inn on the Ocean and Danielle Hanscom of the Brampton Inn, both in Maryland—extraordinary innkeepers all.

For hospitality during the cold, early months of work, I thank Amy Haines for the warmth of Out of the Fire, Ellen and Steve Exelbert for their cozy cottage, and Paul and Candy Milne, of The Oaks. Paul really knows how to cook an oyster. Lydia and Jerry Kaplan offered advice on everything from publishing to medical care. From Fran Neaton came the perfect metaphor for our line of work.

Technical assistance on the manuscript was provided by Peter Strupp of Princeton Editorial Associates. Thanks also to Melissa Kelly and Dale Patchett. Miss Ebbie down at the post office always got the manuscript where it needed to go next. Bill Lippincott provided a quiet place for work.

A basketful of gratitude to Alice Waters, who inspired appreciation for the fruits that flourish all around us wherever we live, the good, the local, and the seasonal—and to the memory of Julia Child. These two extraordinary women graciously taught Hugo and me, on an earlier project, how (and how not) to present a recipe. Appreciation again to the ever-enthusiastic recipe testers, Hugo, Rick, Lucy, Amanda, Ethan, and Linda, along this time with Kurt Weyrauch.

For friendship, the sharing of local ways including a Christmas goose on the doorstep, and so much more, thanks to the best of neighbors, Susie and Scott Kilmon, also Jerry and Julie, Kurt, Paul, Francine, Liisa and her clan, and Captain Iris. Roland Murray was generous with his great store of historical and practical knowledge, a bridge to the region's past. Many thanks to Bryan Arling, through thick and thin and to Barbara Meade, preeminent bibliophile and friend.

An important part of bringing this account to light was played by Susan Koh, Donald Buxton, Philip Webster, and Bernice Michaels of Chesapeake Chamber Music. I am most indebted to Alison Schwartz of ICM, New York, and to Becky Koh, J.P. Leventhal and their colleagues at Black Dog & Leventhal, for their hard work, vision, and tenacity.

Last, a thousand thanks to Tarmy.